# CRICUT /

MW00512547

*Easy to follow Step-by-Step Tutorials to*

*Master your CRICUT Machine today*

**ANITA SPACE**

This document is geared towards providing exact and reliable information in regard to the topic and issue covered. The publication is sold with the idea that the publisher is not required to render accounting, officially permitted, or otherwise, qualified services. If advice is necessary, legal or professional, a practiced individual in the profession should be ordered.

- From a Declaration of Principles which was accepted and approved equally by a Committee of the American Bar Association and a Committee of Publishers and Associations.

The information provided herein is stated to be truthful and consistent, in that any liability, in terms of inattention or otherwise, by any usage or abuse of any policies, processes, or directions contained within is the solitary and utter responsibility of the recipient reader. Under no

circumstances will any legal responsibility or blame be held

against the publisher for any reparation, damages, or monetary loss due to the information herein, either directly or indirectly.

Respective authors own all copyrights not held by the publisher.

The information herein is offered for informational purposes solely and is universal as so. The presentation of the information is without contract or any type of guarantee assurance.

The trademarks that are used are without any consent, and the publication of the trademark is without permission or backing by the trademark owner. All trademarks and brands within this book are for clarifying purposes only and are owned by the owners themselves, not affiliated with this document.

# Contents

# Introduction

So, you just bought the new Cricut Machine, and you have started wondering how to use it? If you have not noticed the Cricut Machine chatter yet, expect to get your minds fully blown.

Time to begin operating on this superior device like a pro who can handle this all. Take every idea to new heights by linking your creative collection to Cricut! The Cricut Maker and Cricut Explore devices are ideal for creators at all levels, from customized paper creations to custom fabric and household decor. They are designed to operate with a wide range of materials, like iron-on, plastic, canvas, tracing paper, cardstock, faux leather, foam, and wood. Explore versatile Cricut blades, and cutting edge Cricut machines, exciting Cricut cartridges, and a large selection of other instruments and materials.

Perhaps you are planning a purchase and would want to read about the characteristics of Cricut and how its iteration varies from earlier models? Okay, you are at the correct place. This book is for beginners and includes projects with Cricut. Here, you will find out whatever you need to know regarding the Cricut

Machine and how you can get the best out of this device. This book will let you know all the information that will allow you to use the machine like an expert within no time.

Card and scrapbook creators were genuinely focused on the initial machines. At least amongst home craftspeople, electronic cutting devices were fairly innovative and offered a better way to do it all by oneself, from anywhere. Today, anything from producing vinyl decals and iron-on transitions to cloth and sewing designs, and even slicing cork is used by Cricut machines.

The Cricut Machine is an electronic system that uses the Cricut Design Space app to cut out and create designs or patterns (this is quite similar to Adobe Illustrator). From paper to fabric to wood and plastic to several more, you can use any resource to create anything you can think up. There are so many wonderful features in the Cricut Unit, and you will have all you need to be the next ultimate DIY Maker!

# Chapter 1: Cricut Machines; the Fundamentals.

A Cricut is a device that helps users to cut and make exquisite and wonderful creations from resources one did not even realize existed. That is the short explanation. The Cricut Maker is like a hybrid of a design plotter and a cutting tool (but with a knife). Users can also emboss, manufacture, and draw folding patterns to make 3D projects, birthday cards, packages, etc., based on the model they have. For people who enjoy crafting and for those who really need to cut a ton of stuff and various kinds of products, the Cricut is a perfect weapon.

In the Cricut model range, the Cricut Maker is the newest and perhaps most sophisticated unit. A broad variety of flat products under 2.4 m width may be cut through it and can also be debossed, graded, and engraved; from fragile materials such as paper to cardstock, fabrics (from chiffon to denim) and vinyl, to harder and stronger materials such as leather; also, certain woods and metals! By lying on 12 x 12' '(or 12' x 24 ") adhesive mats (ranging from 'Soft Grip' to 'Strong Grip, based on the material being used at the moment) and then fed into the cutting process, these products are ready for cutting.

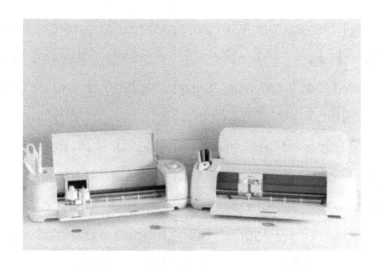

## 1.1 Specifications of Cricut Machine.

• Dimensions: 22.6" x 7.1" x 6.2"

• Weight: 24 lbs.

Cutting Mats Included: 12" x 12" LightGrip Mat and 12" x 12" ClothGrip Pad

Also include: Drive Housing, Rotary Blade and Premium Fine Point Blade and Housing

## 1.2 The best Features.

This elegant unit produces a cutting pressure of 4 kgs, 10X greater than how the Cricut Air sibling provides. The Cricut also sells a USB port, a spinning needle, a blade, and a washable pen.

The cutter also comes with complete access to Cricut's rich sewing design collection in addition to the useful equipment. So, if anyone enjoys stitching as much as they enjoy cutting, this is going to be a big help for him/her. Each of the given sewing design comes as a template of the product you would like to sew. The templates are designed of paper, ensuring that all you have to do is draw your favorite design on the material you plan to use, and the task is almost completed.

Let us presume you are intending on having a tote bag. Two middle panels, two side panels, and a belt will need to be created using a low-end vinyl cutter. Once you print out these designs, before trying to pin them and cutting out all the parts ready for stitching, you would then be expected to draw them onto your cloth. Heck! -Heck! That is very boring and time-consuming as well.

But on the other side, the Cricut Maker, through its Design Space program, facilitates this mission. All you will have to do is plug and play, and the device will do the rest of the thing for you due to this all-new versatility.

But what in particular makes this a cutter worth every penny you invest? Well, here is a closer look at its combination of features.

## The Rotary Blade

For vinyl cutters, there are several explanations of why rotary blades are suggested. The first main explanation is that this style of the blade provides more choices for customization. Therefore, no matter how complicated or twisting your cuts are, you can still rely on this cutter to have a smooth cutting experience. Another advantage of utilizing the Cricut rotatory blade Maker is that you get to experience more accuracy. This is done by the rolling movement of the blades and their gliding expertise.

Out of all the Cricut machines, the rotary blade does not come with all of them, from Explore Air 2, Explore, Personal/V1, and Explore One to Cricut Cake and Cricut Expression. So, to this extent, the Maker evidently enjoys an advantage on almost all of them. As you might know, the requirement for a backer material comparable to further construction versatility is eliminated by this sort of blade. So, Is not it so cool?

## Knife Blade

Are you planning on cutting matboard, chipboard or even balsa? For the task, this really is the blade you will require. The knife blade is the fantasy of any Maker, with the

---

potential to cut through fabrics as dense as 3/32 inches in width. And again, no other Cricut computer besides the Maker, you will not ever find a knife blade. Unnecessary to mention, this blade stays the ideal device for making cuts on dense materials without leaving trace marks.

**Note:** You would need to shift the star wheels on the roller bar in order for it to happen, however.

### Fine Point Blade

The Cricut Maker provides a premium fine-point blade, much like its older siblings, such as the Explore Air series and Explore. This sophisticated blade is capable of creating complex cuts in medium-weighted and thin materials, unlike regular fine point blades (like those used in Personal/V1). Of course, in order to cut your plastic, iron-on, cardstock, and paper, you would need this sort of versatility. Finally, due to its German design, this premium carbide blade can survive wear - and - tear for a long period, enabling creators to experience several hours of working.

### Deep Point Blade

Because Cricut Creator comes with a deep point blade, it becomes something worth enjoying if thick cardstocks have given you a tricky time. Especially in comparison to certain other common blades that provide 45 degrees, this sort of blade has a sharp cutting angle of 60 degrees. There is something else too! It is constructed of sturdy steel and will offer users years of production with no need for a substitute for handcrafted housing.

## Bonded Fabric Blade

It is not necessarily a good decision to gamble with cloth scissors. If you choose to take your job's efficiency a step higher, this specific blade would be a game-changer. It comes with a unique pink color that is supposed to complement the mat with FabricGrip. Bounded Fabric Blade offers us the opportunity to evaluate the sort of fine point blade that is ideally suited to bound fabrics to render those cuts smoother than ever before. In order to create the most out of this blade, you would require an iron-on backer.

## Unique Pens

If the artworks and creations are going to turn out special, pens are what really decide this. So, you should be ready to take advantage of the huge range of pens that come along with the Cricut Maker the next time you attempt to color any pages, create stickers, or prepare decorations for your customers. The Fine Point pen is especially good at making you compose acid-free, water-based illustrations

and draw them. Planning on creating instructional marks on cotton-based cloth for your sewing patterns? The 1.0 tip of the Washable Fabric pen will definitely give you the versatility required to accomplish this task. Some pens included with this device consists:

o Calligraphy

o The Scoring stylus

**Adaptive Tool System**

This useful and modern innovation is another fantastic addition to the Cricut Maker. Effectively, the Agile Toolset gives you the confidence that if other innovations pop up in the future, you will always be able to modify and implement them. It is a major victory here! You do not need to think about other developments that may pop up tomorrow once you buy this device since you will be more than able to handle them. As a quality-conscious consumer, since the Cricut is guaranteed from being redundant in the immediate future, this transforms into more expected earnings.

The Adaptive Tool Device is often used in other Cricut machines, but the one used in the Developer platform is quite distinct. For example, the Maker does this as well

 but with a greater degree of knowledge, while Cricut Explore machines transfer the mat in and out of it and the carriage side-by-side. This is done by the drive housing gears interconnecting with the Adaptive Tool Device gears. A smart and subtle lift that regulates the blade and changes the cut pressure appropriately is the final result.

**Expandable Suite**

It seems that this device's creators created it with the thought of the future.  A strong proof of this would be the extensible suite of instruments. There are various tools inside it, including pens/blades and embossing tools.  And what is more, the computer has amazing extension capacities, so you would be comfortably able to handle them even if different tools pop up again in the future. This vinyl cutter, as it stands, explores the ability to produce much more than papercrafts. So, you can go ahead and produce jewelry, wedding invitations, photo books, and even decorations for a party.

## 1.3 Types of Cricut Machine.

At present, three Cricut machines are commercially available: Cricut Maker, Cricut Explore Air 2, and the relatively new Cricut Joy. It is based on what kind of task you want or need, to decide which Cricut Maker to buy. All Cricut machines have built-in Cricut's free Design Space App.

### Cricut Maker

Cricut Maker is the cutting devices' workhorse. It can do almost everything you want it to. With the Cricut Maker, you may use any blade to carve, engrave, mold, or cut just about any form of carving material. knife-blade, fine-blade, deboss, perforate, engrave, wavy-blade are some of the available blades. Cricut Maker can do much more than other machines of its type. By connecting it to one's device via Bluetooth, one can export his/her own fonts and templates to the Design

Space App for free and then use them.

## Cricut Explore Air 2

A speedy device, the Cricut Explore Air 2, writes and cuts up to 2 times as quick as the earlier Explore Air model. Up to 100 material types, including vinyl, cardstock, and iron-on materials, can be cut by the Explore Air 2. It has two holders for holding tools so that both writing and cutting instruments can be fully prepared. With Bluetooth functionality, users can connect their Bluetooth-enabled device with the Cricut Explore 2 from Design Space. User's fonts and designs can also be uploaded for free!

## Cricut Joy

Transform your ideas into reality with a little assistance from Cricut Joy, your DIY best mate. This clever little writing and cutting machine is incredibly easy to set up and use and lets you make much more of something in less time. You will find yourselves customizing, arranging, and personalizing every other day. Cut vinyl decals for interior decorations or customized water bottles. Create kitchen or office tags easily. Make birthday banners or cards. It also operates without a mat, with Cricut Smart Materials for incredibly, super-long cuts. Cricut Joy makes it simple and convenient to create something special for you or for anyone at a second's notice with various projects that take only 15 to 20 minutes. It is the right partner for Cricut Explore and Cricut Maker devices. It cuts more than 50 materials without a cutting mat, like iron-on, paper, vinyl, fabric, cardstock, and Smart Materials, making super easy and super long cuts. Draw any design and compose it in a number of styles. Cuts specific shapes up to 4 feet long or repeatedly cuts up to 20 feet long.

| WHICH CRICUT IS RIGHT FOR ME? | CRICUT JOY | CRICUT EXPLORE AIR 2 | CRICUT MAKER |
|---|---|---|---|
| MSRP | $179.99 | $249.99 | $399.99 |
| MATERIALS IT CAN CUT | 50+ | 100+ | 300+ |
| MAX MATERIAL WIDTH | 4.5" | 12" | 12" |
| MAX MATERIAL LENGTH | 20' | 24" | 24" |
| **FEATURES** | | | |
| BLUETOOTH ENABLED | ● | ● | ● |
| UPLOAD YOUR OWN IMAGES | ● | ● | ● |
| PRING THEN CUT | | ● | ● |
| CARD MAT FOR CUSTOM CARDS | ● | | |
| MAT-FREE CUTTING | ● | | |
| **BLADES & TOOLS** | | | |
| STANDARD FINE POINT BLADE | ● | ● | ● |
| DEEP CUT BLADE | | ● | ● |
| ROTARY BLADE | | | ● |
| KNIFE BLADE | | | ● |
| SCORING TOOL | | ● | ● |
| DEBOSSING TOOL | | | ● |
| ENGRAVING TOOL | | | ● |
| PERFORATION TOOL | | | ● |
| PEN FOR DRAWING / WRITING | ● | ● | ● |
| **POPULAR MATERIALS** | | | |
| CARDSTOCK AND PAPER | ● | ● | ● |
| ADHESIVE VINYL | ● | ● | ● |
| IRON ON VINYL | ● | ● | ● |
| INFUSIBLE INK | ● | ● | ● |
| BONDED FABRIC | ● | ● | ● |
| FABRIC | | | ● |
| BASSWOOD / BALSA WOOD* | | | ● |
| CRICUT FELT | ● | ● | ● |
| WOOL BLEND FELT* | | | ● |
| CRICUT FAUX LEATHER | ● | ● | ● |
| CRICUT GENUINE LEATHER | | ● | ● |
| TOOLING / GARMENT LEATHER | | | ● |

## 1.4 Why Better than Other Machines?

This is a costly affair to have a Cricut machine, and several times, the stuff people choose to make with the device can be achieved by cutting with hands.

But the time this little device would save for you would be enough to start a new project. The amount of sophistication of cuts users can create makes the fantasy of any crafter come true. And when they mix them with the latest equipment and customized designs, the opportunities for production are simply wonderful.

Another aspect of Cricut's latest machines that distinguish them from other machines is that they can cut and draw simultaneously. They have slots for a blade and a pen both. Cricut Machine would be a big time-saver If you are creating cards and especially such ones that require any of these functions.

## 1.5 Where to Find Cricut Machine.

You can directly purchase the Cricut Machine from the Cricut's website or buy them from sites like Amazon. On Ebay and Craiglist, certain older versions can be ordered, but they are more challenging to get a hold of.

## 1.6 Is Cricut Machine too expensive?

Let's inform you straight away that YES, Cricut machine can be pretty expensive.

Note that I said it "can be." This is because you will see that

there are indeed decent prices as you glance at any of the first machines, and you can get started as quickly as you choose.

The Cricut Cuttlebug, a small but efficient die cutting machine, is the least expensive machine and the most expensive choice is their new release, The Cricut Maker.

## 1.7 Does it print?

Strictly speaking, the Cricut machine does not print, but one can use the pen holder rather than the cutting blade (or one can also use both simultaneously depending on one's Cricut Model)

This helps to create printable pictures or to make images on paper using various color markers.

They, too, have a marker for washable fabric, which can be used prior to cutting, to label the fabric.

## 1.8 Does it need ink?

For using your Cricut, you do not require ink as Cricut Machine does not print. If you are choosing the drawing option however, to be able to draw with it, you need Cricut pens. They have a wide selection of choices for you to pick from.

## 1.9 Does it embross?

The Cricut Cuttlebug is the only Cricut Machine which was and is capable of truely embossing.

Get an adapter, swap the blade housing with this adapter, attach your scoring stylus, and instruct Cricut Design Space to cut if you choose to use your Cricut for embossing. It will be embossed then!

## 1.10 Does it sew?

No, Cricut does not sew, and it is too easy to believe that it does. This is because if you are a sewer, you would have heard all the good stories about it. But Cricut Maker's managing of designs is among its most jaw-dropping features. It has the potential to directly translate all the template markings onto your fabrics, so you can never skip a mark. Design Space will also inform you which way your fabric should be moving whenever you load your mats. And with only a few taps, Cricut Maker marks and cuts your design, which means you are going to get plenty of time to concentrate on the enjoyable part, which is sewing the fabric.

## 1.11 Can we use any pens with the cricut machine?

Cricut provides a wide range of pens that you can buy, and which fit in the holder of the machine. To use Cricut pens, the Explore One machine needs a separate adapter.

Thanks to a dual tool holder, the Cricut Explore machine provides the opportunity to cut a design and use the pen simultaneously.

Also, certain pen brands fit into the same adapter as the Cricut pens:

- American Crafts Galaxy Markers
- American Crafts Slick Writers
- American Crafts Precision Pens
- Tombow twin tone

- Crayola Markers, thin tips

- Pilot Precise V5 Pens

- American Crafts Glitter Markers

- Recollections Markers

## 1.12 What Materials can the Cricut Machine cut?

You can cut various materials with the Cricut machines. Among the most common are:

- Posterboard

- Cardstock

- Iron-On

- Paper

- Vinyl

Wood. Of all the available cutting machines by Cricut. It is only the Cricut Maker that can cut wood. Balsa and basswood are some of the wood forms you can cut with a Cricut Machine. You need to take into consideration that wood cannot be cut with the regular blade that comes with the Cricut Maker. You would need the Knife Blade for these types of projects, a form of blade specially crafted to cut such thick materials.

- Fabric. The Cricut would be your strongest and most reliable cutting assistant if you deal with fabrics and need to cut lots of cloth of multiple sizes. The Cricut maker helps you to cut fabric easily. So, if your profession is sewing, then this is the best reason for you to get a Cricut. Investing in Cricut will always be worth it. With the Cricut Explore machines, you can cut fabric, but the need to sew it remains.

## 1.13 Its Accessories.

The Cricut machine comes with almost everything you nee d to set up and make the        sample project. Do you want to know what is inside the Cricut box?

Here is the list:

- Materials for your first projects

- Rotary Blade and Drive Housing

- Fine Point Pen

- LightGrip Mat 12" x 12'

- USB cable

- A Cricut Access free trial membership

- Cricut Maker Machine

- Premium Fine Point Blade and Housing

- FabricGrip Mat 12" x 12"

- Welcome book

- Power adapter

- 50 free ready-to-make projects, which includes 25 sewing patterns

## 1.14 What Is Cricut Infusible Ink and Cricut Infusible Ink Transfers?

Basically, Cricut Infusible Ink is an ink transfer tool. The transfer sheets are made up of dry ink product, and the ink is directly injected onto the base material as high heat is applied. Basically, you dye the base material instead of placing a coating on top of the base material (like iron-on vinyl). Cricut Infusible Ink is a new innovative DIY product range that helps you to make customized, expert transitions on t-shirts, coasters, tote bags, and much more.

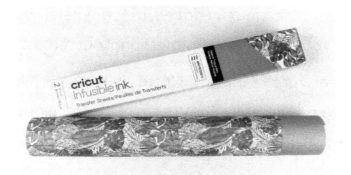

While this may sound like vinyl or iron-on but infusible Ink is quite different. With Infusible Ink, the craft becomes a part of the product instead of the craft lying on top of a product. This makes a huge difference. This ensures you get colors that are bright and do not peel, wrinkle, flake, or crack. Without fading, the vivid colors last even after washing multiple times. Through Infusible Ink, you can pull on a shirt, and it stretches along with the cloth because it has been infused into the fabric. It is completely incredible because you can achieve professional outcomes!

The transfers look a little like Cricut's other vinyl sheets, but they act very differently. They seem more like thick paper or adhesive vinyl than the regular iron-on. The transfers are available in:

- Solid: 2 pack consisting 12" x 12" sheets. Price: $12.99

- Pattern: variety 2 pack consisting 12" x 12" sheets Price: $12.99

- Pattern: variety 4 pack consisting 12" x 12" sheets. Price: $17.99

Remember that the colors of the transition sheet seem even less vivid than the finished project would turn out to be. For Example, the transfer sheets appear almost brown in case it is solid green. But once moved, they will be bright green.

## 1.15 What are cricut mats.

To enable you to cut a number of different materials quickly, the Cricut cutting mats have already been designed. To help you distinguish them, each of them has a different grip (or extent of stickiness) and color.

These mats come in 2 different sizes, which are:

- 12 x 12 in

- 12 x 24 in

To preserve your mats in the best condition, keep the clear cover when storing it and, when possible, use a scraper to scrape off excess pieces and a spatula to remove cut pieces.

**LightGrip machine mat:** LightGrip machine mat can be used with the Cricut Explore and Cricut Maker family and are suitable for lighter materials. These are blue in color. These mats are ideal for:

- Thin cardstock

- Printer paper

- Vellum

- Vinyl

- Construction paper

**StandardGrip machine mat:** StandardGrip machine mats can also be used with the Cricut Explore family and the Cricut Maker. These are green in color. These mats are suitable for a large variety of medium-weight items, ideal for:

- Embossed cardstock

- Cardstock

- Pattern paper

- Vinyl

- Iron-on

**StrongGrip machine mat:** StrongGrip machine mat can also be used for the Cricut Explore family and Cricut Maker. These are purple in color and are suitable for heavyweight materials and are ideal for:

- Magnet material

- Glitter cardstock

- Thick cardstock

- Chipboard

- Posterboard

- Leather

- Fabric with stabilizer

**FabricGrip machine mat:** FabricGrip machine mat is a special mat that has more strength and density. Besides, it has a light adhesive suitable for a large range of fabrics. This mat is pink in color. It was designed to be used with the Bonded-fabric blade or the Rotary blade.

## 1.16 what are cricut smart set dial?

The Smart Set dial is a dial for material selection that provides pre-defined settings on vinyl, poster board, paper, cardstock, iron-on, canvas, and more to get the outstanding outcome. The Smart Set dial removes the need for us to make adjustments in depth, manual pressure, and speed. The "Custom" settings on the Smart Set dial helps you to pick or create your own 'custom setting' with pre-programmed custom material. You can set the dial to 'Custom' and then click 'Make It' from Design Space App when you are cutting a material that is not specified on the Smart Set Dial. You may pick the material from the cut preview screen if it is specified in the drop-down menu.

Users can add a new custom material to their Design Space App from either the Cut Screen or the Design Space Account menu. (the option only appears if the dial is set to Custom). In the iOS mobile app, adding new material is only accessible via the Account menu.

You can add new material to the Custom Materials screen by pressing the 'Add New Material' button (Windows/Mac) or by hitting the '+' button in the upper right corner of the Design Space screen. You may have to specify:

- Material's name (on Windows/Mac, after naming the material, press Save to use the following options).

- The Cut pressure by using the slider or +/- keys.

- Multicut (this makes Cricut cut multiple times over the same design - specifically used for thick materials)

- Type of Blade (Deep Point or Premium Fine Point so that Design Space can prompt you according to blade type)

Once they are set up, to save the latest custom material, press Save and then Done.

## 1.17 What is cricut easy press?

An EasyPress machine is a small heating device that enables HTV (Heat Transfer Vinyl), Iron-On, or infusible ink designs to be quickly transferred to the preferred surface. HTV and Iron-On are the materials that need to be heated to enable and achieve a good transfer on the glue side. To satisfy various surfaces and uses, Cricut offers EasyPress in 4 different sizes.

Cricut EasyPress 6 x 7 in: This is the smaller version of the standard EasyPress style; 3.3 lb in weight is ideal for tiny flat projects:

o Beanies

o Baby clothes

o Small bags

o Socks

o Gloves

**Cricut EasyPress 9 x 9 inches**: This easy press is of medium size. It is the best size for most tasks and perhaps the most recommended if you are an EasyPress beginner. It weighs just 5.7lb. It performs well for projects such as:

o Pillows

o Tote bags

o T-shirt

o Apron

**Cricut EasyPress 10 x 12 inches**: This is the EasyPress's largest size and is suitable for bigger projects in which you need a relatively larger area to transfer, such as:

o Blankets

o Big T-shirts

o Large projects

o Sweatshirts

**Cricut EasyPress Mini**: This is Cricut's new release, and it is the ideal shape for tiny projects in challenging places or surfaces, such as:

o Baseball caps

o Shoes

o Small non-flat clothes

## 1.18 What are Cricut Blades and what do these blades do?

**Knife Blade:**

This only works for Cricut Maker. This stunning little blade will cut very dense materials such as basswood. This blade makes the Cricut Maker an ideal machine to create.

With this little thing, the projects you can cut are just fantastic. You can make boxes, wood signs, incredibly durable cake toppers, and more for your house. The mat you can use for this blade is the StrongGrip Mat, the purple one. Often the mat is not sufficient to hold the materials in position, particularly when you cut wood. Use the painter's tape on its sides to hold it to the mat if you need to apply an additional grip.

**Rotary Blade:**

Only works for Cricut Maker. The Rotary blade is amazing, and the Adaptive Tool System drives it, so it is only compatible with Cricut Maker. This blade's drive housing is not interchangeable with the other types of blades. You require a specific kit for you to adjust the blade itself. The Rotary blade cuts into quite a number of materials. And most of all, no backing material is required to hold the fabric on the mat. That itself can make you super delighted! The Cricut Maker often comes with this blade (this is a huge deal since you typically have to purchase these kinds of instruments individually or in a bundle), which can only be used with Fabric-Grip Mat. Although this blade is very good and efficient, there is a slight restriction on it. At least 3/4 of an inch of the design or project size you are attempting to cut should be 19 mm. Cutting smaller designs can result in the life of the blade being reduced.

## Deep point blade:

The Deep Point blade would be your best companion whenever you choose to cut tougher materials. With either of the Cricut Maker or Cricut Explore Family, you will use it. The angle of the deep point blade is much steeper, i.e., 60 degrees, which is 45 degrees for the fine point blade, enabling the blade for penetrating in dense materials. This blade is black in color, and it must be used with its corresponding housing. By that, it means that other knives, including the Fine Point blade and Bonded Fabric blade, could not be interchanged.

## Bonded Fabric Blade:

The Bonded Fabric blade is much similar to the Fine Point Blade, except that it is color-coded since you can only use it for fabric. Do not use this blade on vinyl or paper to get a great fabric cutting experience. For this blade, however, there is a major warning. It is important to bind the cloth that you may cut to a backing material.

You may know what bonded fabric is if you are a sewer, but if you do not have any direct experience with the fabrics, let us describe it to you pretty quickly. The color is pink, and it can be used with the Pink Fabric Mat and Fine Point blade housing. The bonded fabric blade is compatible with the Cricut Maker and Explore Family Machines. You can also do that for the Standard Green Mat, if you do not have the pink mat.

**Perforation Blade:**

Quick Swap Perforation blade: This unique blade will allow you to build projects incredibly well. A whole universe of possibilities has opened up with this tool. It just functions with the Cricut Maker.

Quick Swap Wavy blade: This tool can create wavy patterns on the final cuts rather than cutting straight lines like the fine point or rotatory blade. It just functions with the Cricut Maker

Quick Swap Debossing tip: This tip will drive the material in, and stunning and intricate designs will be created. Because of the details that you apply to your creations, the debossing would carry your creations to a new level. It only functions with Cricut Maker.

Quick Swap Engraving tip: The Engraving Tip is the thing a lot of crafters have been searching for. Users will be capable of engraving a broad range of materials with this tool. It only functions with the Cricut Maker.

Quick Swap Scoring Wheel tips: The Scoring Wheel is an instrument that helps users to make elegant, crispy, and edgy folds. It only functions with the Cricut Maker.

**Foil Transfer Kit:**

The "Foil Transfer Kit" enables you to make crisp foil and elegant effects on your projects. It is compatible with Cricut Explore family machines and the Cricut Maker. Foil Transfer kit is 3 in 1; Cricut also has fine, bold, and medium tips that will best suit your project.

| | Premium Fine-Point Blade | Deep-Point Blade | Bonded-Fabric Blade | Rotary Blade | Knife Blade |
|---|---|---|---|---|---|
| Maker | ✓ | ✓ | ✓ | ✓ | ✓ |
| Explore | ✓ | ✓ | ✓ | | |
| Explore One | ✓ | ✓ | ✓ | | |
| Explore Air | ✓ | ✓ | ✓ | | |
| Explore Air Z | ✓ | ✓ | ✓ | | |

## 1.19 What can you make and sell with Cricut Machine?

With your Cricut, there are also opportunities for earning money, which includes selling personalized t-shirts, decals, mugs, etc., online or at art shows. Cricut machines are dyeing and cutting machines. Depending on the machine you are using, you can cut a vast range of materials. Materials like cardstock, paper, cardboard, vinyl, and many more can be cut by Cricut Explore Air. There are many more choices for the Cricut Maker, like several fabric varieties, leather, and thin wood. As well as having scoring lines, Cricut machines often have the capacity to create images and text. You will find a comprehensive list on Cricut's website about what can each type of Cricut machine cut.

The Cricut machines are capable of working with a broad variety of products, which ensures there are lots of options for usage. For scrapbooking, greeting cards, customizing T-shirts, or papercrafts with iron-on patterns, many crafters enjoy using Cricut machines. Another common use of Cricut for vinyl decals is creating custom tumblers and mugs. The party's decor, personalized posters, stickers, wall art, and the list has no end.

- Home Decoration: Decals for windows and walls. Or personalize things like baskets, frames or even cooking spices.

- Stickers: for journaling, planning and much more.

- Greeting Cards: Users can create greeting cards. Like those you see in the market.

- Clothing Items: Cut and iron on elegant and customized designs on T-Shirts.

- 3D Projects: Gift boxes, paper toys and 3D greeting cards.

- With the help of Cricut Maker, users can cut wood and make 3D and solid projects.

- Users can also cut fabric and make fashion items for their clothing.

- One's imagination is the limit.

Users can sell up to 10,000 completed projects a year using Cricut goods and any of their copyrighted content under the Cricut Angel Policy. Works incorporating copyright material must contain a note that reads "Includes Cricut's Copyright Material." However, some big corporations such as Sesame, Entertainment One UK Limited, Disney, Hello Kitty, Martha Stewart, Warner Bros, Airstie Allsop, and the Boy Scouts of America do not offer products using copyrighted materials.

## 1.20 Is it worth buying for a common person like sewist?

First, there are tons of ready-to-make and personalized exclusive sewing projects and digital templates available from designers such as Riley Blake and Simplicity inside Cricut Design Space / Access. As you might easily assume, these are smaller projects that would work on your mats (as no pattern design can be larger than the size of mat). In order to correctly piece the parts of the project together, they must be cut precisely and sometimes identically.

For other people, when deciding whether a Cricut is worth it for you or not, your own design skills are certainly not a consideration!  You can indeed design your own graphics and images with your computer or any machine, but you can also get loads of pre-designed graphics, images, and projects with Cricut. Cricut machines are durable and their quality is really incredible.

## 1.21 What are cricut cartridges and do you need them?

Cricut cartridges are a series of photos you can obtain and use on your Cricut machine to make projects.

These collections are based on a season, a theme, a holiday, licensed characters, types, etc. Typically, there is a common thread that links all the photos on a particular cartridge together. These Cricut cartridges were typically genuine physical little plastic cartridges you could plug into your Cricut Machine cartridge slot.

In reality, using cartridges with the earlier Cricut machines was common (before the Explore family of Cricut machines). You may not need to purchase physical Cricut cartridges whether you have Cricut Explore series machines or a Cricut Maker. In Cricut Access, you can purchase these picture sets, or if you have a membership, several would already be provided for you to use.

Let us assume someone gifted you a huge box of their old cartridges that worked for them. Or you may only keep searching about them because you really are not aware of what they're used for. All those old cartridges will undoubtedly be used for some of the Cricut electronic legacy Machines (no longer marketed by Cricut); for instance, the Expression series will use the cartridges as they still do through manually putting them into the system and using the keyboard overlay, or by linking them to the Cricut Craft Room. All these cartridges can still be used by the newer devices, the Cricut Maker and the Cricut Explore Series. You have to connect them to your Cricut account first, though, so you can browse them online using Cricut Design Space.

These cartridges or picture sets can be linked to your Cricut ID and accessed online via Cricut Craft Room (Expression series) or Cricut Design Space (Explore series). You can also buy digital cartridges, view the internet for image collections without thinking about working with any physical cartridges. For an inexperienced crafter, cartridges are a fantasy. It can be fantastic to make your own designs from scratch, but it is often a little daunting to look at a blank canvas and wonder where to start. You can quickly find motivation with cartridges at hand, divided by every holiday or theme you can think up. Without wasting ages obsessing about the template, cartridges are a convenient and straightforward way to plunge into making DIY greeting cards and vinyl decals.

You will find lots of step-by-step instructions for creating cartridge creations. When you are first practicing how to use a Cricut, these are nice to use. When you start, there are too many different topics to master. Tutorials make it easier by cutting out all the guesswork!

## Pros

o The images are deliberately chosen and well-curated in each cartridge. Many creative designers have spent lots of time and money only for you to use in making projects! It would help if you were assured that the graphics and fonts would be of acceptable quality and function with your Cricut smoothly.

o The Cricut Cartridge Collection includes nearly 500 hundred cartridges! There are numerous projects and images in each cartridge that can be edited and mixed with various artistic characteristics, offering an exceptional variety of designs. You will still find something that looks perfect with any project you make. There are only too many forms, designs, and fonts to pick from.

o In fact, cartridges are of great importance. You may create hundreds of numerous designs from the raw images from only a single cartridge. If you feel that your stock of Cricut cartridges has become too pricey, spend more time playing with the cartridges you already have, and make fair use of that innovative value.

o It would be great to have a tangible set of Cricut cartridges to find your next project's motivation. You should keep off the internet and search through an extensive library with your cartridge set instead of trying to gaze through pictures on a screen to locate anything to create.

## Cons

o The cartridge scheme's biggest limitation until the Cricut Explore sequence was that you were restricted to what came on those cartridges. With the newest Cricut devices, as cartridges are now entirely optional, this is no more a drawback! You can still share your own drawings or use SVGs that you find online for free.

o One big problem is that you can only link cartridges to a single account with Cricut. If a cartridge is connected to a Cricut account, it is permanently connected. A cartridge may not be unlinked or moved to another account. Also, they can already be connected to someone else's account whether you are gifted cartridges or purchase any from e-bay or a thrift store! It is permanent to connect cartridges, and you cannot switch whose account they are connected to. So, make sure you do not get fooled into getting cartridges that your Cricut cannot really use.

o You may sometimes feel like you are stuck into the Cricut

o brand, or maybe even with a specific machine, after purchasing a bunch of cartridges. For Cricut, this is fine, but not so nice for sharing with the crafting and DIY groups. You cannot freely swap your ideas with other individuals if you work with cartridges, one of the best aspects of designing new projects! They can be conveniently exchanged with others and imported into the modeling applications for other cutter companies, such as Silhouette Studio if you use regular ol 'SVG files instead.

o For each Cricut machine, cartridges do not function the same. You will use cartridges without the internet in the Expressions. For the Cricut Explore Air 2, the cartridge must be connected to your account. And there is not even a cartridge space in the Cricut Maker! If you want to use photos with a Maker from all your old cartridges, you will have to buy Cricut's special Cartridge Adapter to connect them.

# Chapter 2: Cricut Machines; Working and Maintenance.

## 2.1 Setting up your cricut machine.

Completing the system configuration would immediately register your account for the machine. Follow these measures to set up your Cricut Explore, Explore Air, Explore 1, Explore Maker, and Cricut Explore Air 2 machine:

- Plug in your Cricut Machine and switch it on.

- Connect your Machine to your whatever device (computer, mobile etc.) with a USB cable or connect it through Bluetooth.

- Search design.cricut.com/setup in your device's browser.

- Download and then install the Design Space for your Desktop.

- Follow the instructions that are shown on your screen to sign-in and create your Cricut ID, and then set up your machine.

- You will get to know the setup is finished when you are asked to do a test cut.

Note: Your machine would be auto registered during the set-up. If you did not finish setup the first time you linked your machine with your computer or mobile, reconnect your system, go to design.cricut.com/setup, or click New Machine Setup from the Design Space Account panel, and obey the instructions on the screen.

## 2.2 How to find projects to make from Cricut?

Cricut Design Space is one of the easiest ways to locate designs and cut files from Cricut. If you make anything from scratch or use a pre-designed idea, this is where all Cricut programs begin. Registering a Cricut Design Space account is easy, so you can do that to discover all the possible designs or work from home on a project. However, most of the pre-designed project files from Cricut cost money to use, unless you have a Cricut Access subscription.

You can also use your own .gif, .jpg, .png, .svg .bmp, and .dxf images by uploading on the Design Space app. On platforms such as Etsy, you can use photos you have or buy cut files and then add them to the app. It is not as challenging as it looks to import images into the Design Space! On their website, Cricut has given some simple guidance on how to do it.

## 2.3 How does it work?

You may wirelessly attach a Cricut to your device, generate or import designs on your computer, and upload them for cutting on your Cricut. Cricut has applications named Design Space (it is available for MAC, Windows, and mobile phones) that helps you to build and import cut designs. A small blade (pen, rotary cutter, or scoring tool) is installed within the Cricut. You will attach your preferred material to a 12-inch large cutting mat until you have a template ready to cut in Design Space, submit your design to your Cricut wirelessly from your phone, and then mount your item to your machine. You will begin cutting your project with the click of a button.

## 2.4 Is it easy to use?

YES, for the most part.

BUT it depends, mainly if you are not a really tech-savvy individual, there is certainly a learning process. Cricut machines come with a detailed online manual, and there are a number of other online Cricut tools, but they are pretty easy to learn how to use. Both the Cricut machine and Design Space are designed to be really user-friendly, and you do not need a lot of expertise with graphic design to use them (though it does assist if you want to make your own designs from scratch). In Cricut's Design Room, there is a library of photos and designs that are easy to import as a fresh project. Some are complimentary, and some can be ordered at a reduced discount.

## 2.5 Do all blades work with all machines?

New blades have been launched by Cricut, which are only compatible with Cricut Maker.

But why? A modern cutting method, the adaptive tool system, is used by the Cricut Maker, which enables the unit to be ten times more powerful!

Each machine you buy contains a blade. Following are the blades and their models:

- Cricut Explore Air: Fine-Point blade.

- Cricut Explore One: Fine-Point blade.

- Cricut Maker: Fine-Point blade and a Rotary blade.

- Cricut Explore Air 2: Fine-Point blade.

## 2.6 Is there a need of an alternative software?

There was actually a way for users to do it with third-party software, but it is not applicable for the newer Cricut

Machines.

What you can do is design what you need to cut on Illustrator and then cut it from your printer. But whether it is just basic shapes or texts, Cricut Design Space is always enough.

## 2.7 Can to connect Cricut it with Bluetooth or computer?

Not actually, though Cricut Design SpaceTM is computer-based, Windows and Mac-compatible software. Only Mac operating systems and windows are compatible with the Cricut Design Space. In other terms, to use Cricut Machines, you need to have a desktop computer.

- You have to use the Cricut Design Space software to use your device without the Internet. This application is convenient and links with Bluetooth. This app is only accessible for iOS users, iPhone users, and Apple users. Most smart devices and tablets are consistent with the Cricut Design Space Application. They have launched an Android model, and you could link wirelessly through Bluetooth and cut off your computer based on the system you have.

- Bluetooth Included: Each has built-in Bluetooth technologies for Explore Air2, Cricut Maker, and Cricut Explore. So, with your desktop computer or mobile device, you can connect to them.

- Ensure that your Cricut Explore or Cricut Maker machine is turned on and within 10-15 feet of your computer. Guarantee that the Wireless Bluetooth Connector is inserted whether you have an Explore or Explore One.

- Determine if your PC is Bluetooth activated by accessing the Device Manager and checking for a Bluetooth Radios section. If there is no Bluetooth radio on your computer, Bluetooth is not available. To enable your computer to speak to other Bluetooth devices, you may need to buy a USB gadget called a Bluetooth Dongle.

- Control the Control Panel Devices and Printer window. Click Add a device" (or "Add a device with Bluetooth").

- Enable your Wireless Bluetooth Adapter to be sensed by the PC or Explore Air, Explore Air 2, or Bluetooth module Cricut Maker.

- To open the pairing options, pick the adapter/Bluetooth module name and press it two times.

- Pick "Enter the pairing code of the device" and type 0000 into the slot. Select "Next The pairing between your Cricut adapter and PC is now complete. To shut the browser, press 'Close.'

- BLUETOOTH ADAPTER NEEDED: The Cricut Explore and the Cricut Explore One require a **Wireless Bluetooth adapter** to be able to cut wirelessly.

**Pairing with a Mac Computer**:

- Make sure your computer is within 10-15 feet of your Cricut Maker machine or Cricut Explore. Ensure that the Wireless Bluetooth Connector is inserted whether you have an Explore or Explore One.

- Determine if your Mac is equipped with Bluetooth by opening System Preferences and searching for the Bluetooth option.

- Open a window on Bluetooth. If the Bluetooth service is deactivated, press the button to turn it on. From the system list, pick the Cricut Maker Bluetooth module, Wireless Bluetooth, Explore Air 2, or Explore Air. (The packaging materials include the name of your Wireless Bluetooth Adapter.) To start the pairing process, press Pair. Enter the code 0000 when requested and press Pair.

- Your Bluetooth® Wireless Adapter is already paired with your Mac.

**Pairing with an iOS Device:**

- Make sure that your Cricut Explore or Cricut Maker computer is turned ON and within 10-15 feet of your iOS unit. Ensure that the Wireless Bluetooth Connector is inserted whether you have an Explore or Explore One.

- Open the Software for Settings.

- Tap it to turn it on if your Bluetooth contact is switched off. In the list, you can see the name of the Cricut Explore Wireless Bluetooth Adapter or your Explore Air2, Explore Air, or Cricut Maker Bluetooth module. (In your packing products, you can notice the name of your adapter.)

- From the list to be partnered with, pick your adapter/Bluetooth module title. As shown by the progress spinner, your iOS computer will start the pairing process. For the PIN, type 0000 when requested, and then click Done.

- A new page will appear asking for your permission to allow Cricut Design Space and your computer to interact. Choose the permitted alternative to go on. The Cricut Design Space software will then be routed to you. You already have your iOS computer matched with your Cricut Explore Wireless Bluetooth Adapter, Explore Air 2, Explore Air, or Cricut Maker.

**Pairing with an Android Device:**

- Make sure that your Cricut Explore or Cricut Maker computer is turned ON and within 10-15 feet of your iOS unit. Ensure that the Wireless Bluetooth Connector is inserted whether you have an Explore or Explore One.

- Open the Settings application that can be opened

  from the Apps screen or, if appropriate, by swiping from the screen's top.

- Press Bluetooth from the window's left pane. Tap it to turn it on if your Bluetooth connectivity is off. In the list, you can see the name of the Cricut Explore Wireless Bluetooth Adapter for either your Explore Air 2, Explore Air, or Cricut Maker Bluetooth module. (In your shipping products, you can see the name of your adapter. You will see the name of your Explore Air, Air 2, or Cricut Maker Bluetooth unit on a tag on the bottom of the machine.

- Pick from the list the name of your adapter/Bluetooth module. Your Android device will trigger the linking phase. Type 0000 or 1234 for the PIN when requested, then tap Finished.

- The Cricut device will be seen under "Paired Devices" when the pairing phase is complete and can be used with the Cricut Design Space Android App to complete a cut.

## 2.8 Maintenance

### Cleaning Cricut Machines

o Wipe the external panels carefully with a

   slightly wet cloth.

o Dry any residual moisture instantly with a soft fabric or chamois.

o Do not try to use any chemicals (including, though not only, carbon tetrachloride, acetone, and benzene) or alcohol-based cleaning products on the machine. It would help if you also prevent scratchy cleansers and washing equipment. Do not dip the system or any part of it in water.

o  Remember not to eat food or drink when using the machine, and keep the machine away from sweets and drinks.

o  Keep it in a safe, dust-free spot.

o  Do not leave the system in a car, where extreme heat will melt or damage the plastic parts, to prevent unnecessary heat or cold.

o  Do not open in intense sunlight for a prolonged period.

**Caring for the Cutting Mat**

o  The Cricut Cutting Mat can be expected to be used anywhere from 25-40 complete mat cuts until a replacement is needed.

o  Based on the setting you use and the material you cut, the real cutting mat life expectancy can vary.

o  If the paper does not hold to the cutting mat anymore, it is time to fix it.

o  Using just authentic Cricut replacement is always advised.

## 2.9 Some Basic tips.

- Flip the project face down and push the mat away from the material as it is time to remove the completed project from the mat, rather than attempting to remove the product from the mat. In the removal process, this prevents the material from being curled.

- It may be hard to get tiny bits of vinyl or paper out of a design. For very tiny stuff, try a safety pin.

- Dip the weeding tool into the tacky and use it more easily to dig up the pieces.

- Before using your pricey, fancy, once-of-a-kind stuff, always evaluate your cuts on scrap material. It is going to save you money and a headache!

- If you cut incredibly tough or dense stuff, the Cricut would possibly cut it many times. What if it was not enough to cut through all the way? Again, cut it! Hold the mat in place (do not click the arrow button to eject it and re-press the "C" (Go) button, it will cut it again!

- Use an inkjet printer as you print and cut. It appears to operate a lot more than a laser printer. The calibration light used for picking up the registration marks will heat the toner and make the machine not read it. You can use an inkjet printer from HP, which really fits excellent for printing and cutting.

- If you try to use print and cut on something other than white paper, the registration markings would definitely not be able to be understood by Cricut. So instead of printing white paper registration marks, cut them out and stick them over the non-white paper before sticking it in your Cricut! On sticker paper, cut these registration markers out and place them over the marks on the colored paper.

- • Use Chrome or Safari Internet Explorer browsers that allow photos up to 6.75" wide x 9.256" large, if you choose the full file size to be included for the Print and Cut functionality. (Only photos up to 5.5" wide and 8.5' high are enabled by Firefox.)

- Had trouble putting your non-Cricut pen in the correct writing position? When you insert your ink, put a craft stick under clamp A, stopping just as the pen touches the craft stick. Close the loop, take the art stick out, and it will be in the ideal position for your design.

- Try wrapping tape around the barrel, so it fits snugly if you choose to use another ink, but it is too small. Electrical tape does a good job.

- In the built-in accessory cup, store your pen's cap so that your ink remains close to the tip, always ready to use!

- If you make your own projects, the score line on the canvas can be doubled for stronger and deeper scores.

- Spread a strip of aluminum foil on your mat if your blade does not cut as quickly as it did, then cut a basic pattern into it. It is going to make the blade sharpen a little. This is quite effective.

- Try using a blade apart from the blade you use for cutting vinyl to cut paper; it can prolong the blade's existence and allow better cuts. Color code the blades by spraying some acrylic paint on the plastic blade's tip: black for vinyl and white for paper etc.

- Try to stop Google Chrome if you have trouble utilizing Cricut Design Space. The two of them do not play as well together as Safari. Also, Firefox seems to perform better.

- In Cricut Design Room, pay close attention to the layer order since the Cricut would first cut from the bottom layer and go from there. It is also smart to place the broad outlines as the upper layer so that they are completed last, which stops the stuff from being cut out and slipping about when the Cricut already cuts the fine details.

- Try utilizing clear contact paper to take the vinyl off the paper backing rather than the costly transfer papers.

- Tired of your vinyl rolls going loose and unwinding? Use cardboard rolls of paper towel or toilet paper; just cut a long slice from the cardboard and put it over your vinyl roll.

## 2.10 Do's and Do nots

Now is time to make sure that your investment is well taken care of, right? Our Cricut Explore machines do seem to get a little dirty with all the vinyl cutting, glitter paper cutting, cardstock cutting, and other products everyone uses. In conclusion, there are a few strategies that you should use in order to keep your Cricut Explore clean and lovely.

**DO's:**

o Turn off your machine when you are cleaning it.

o Always use a soft cloth for wiping down the machine. You can use a non-alcohol baby wipe as well.

- For removing residue clean off the rollers. You can watch videos on YouTube for tutorial.

- Clean up blade housing for removing the residue. It is important to keep this area neat and clean all the time.

- It is okay to gently move your Cricut's housing unit to one side for cleaning the case.

## DO NOTS:

- Never ever spray any cleaner directly on the machine.

- Never ever wipe off the bar which holds the housing. The grease is needed to be over there.

- Never ever touch the gear chain which is at the back of the machine.

- Do not clean while your machine is switched on to avoid problems.

You can call Cricut Help at 1-877-727-4288 if you find your Cricut Explore is creating a grinding noise. If you need to apply more grease on the housing unit bar, they will

examine it and approve it. They have a special package and directions to use which they will send you. Do not only consider applying some other oil to the bar.

## 2.11 Some fun facts

- Your kitchen organization will now become Pinterest-worthy.

- Do you remember all the adorable jar labels that you have been pinning since 2013? Now you can make some. And you can modify them as much as you want. But spoiler note, you best believe that when your girlfriends see what you have done in your kitchen, they are going to invite you to come over and mark theirs too. Let the Parties of the Cricuts start!

- Any brilliant kitchen organizing start-up ventures are printing labels for plain pantry boxes, drawer labels of a refrigerator.

- A dedicated craft space is required.

o The Maker is a chunky piece of machinery, and to operate it, you will need a decent workspace. Now is the time to cut out a place you never know what to do with before in the random nook in your dining or guest room. Even if it is only a little closet-like mine, all your craft stuff is certainly worth having in one accessible place.

- You will need *ALL* the items.

- Cricut has several sweet gadgets in contrast to the Maker, which can make your creations much smoother, quicker, simpler, and more impressive looking.

- The perfect option to add is BrightPad. It practically resembles a tablet-shaped lightbox that designers use for tracing, and while you are making delicate cuts, it makes weeding so much more uncomplicated.

- The Essential Package, the Portable Trimmer, and the Extra Wide Self-Healing Cutting Pad are strongly recommended. For every project, use these things. Take it from the person who cannot cut a straight line to save Its life, just like a bread knife, and any scissor cut is jagged... whether you were born with tweezers in one hand and straight edge in other, place these tool kits on your wish list for Mother's Day.

- Weeding is addictive!

- Only because weeding is so enjoyable, you are going to catch yourself doing more creations. Although it is a skill that needs practice, it is just a perfect way to relax and de-stress. It is like a game without an irritating buzzer, Operation.

- If you are as fascinated with weeding, three main design Space fonts need a great deal of it:

- For a timeless look: CASTELLAR CASTELLAR

- CHEERFUL SHAPE: For a pleasant vibe.

- ITC RENNIE MACKINTOSH COM LIGHT For a new feeling:

- Potentially grab a BrightPad. It will make it much more enjoyable weeding.

• The Maker performs more than cutting and scoring alone.

- One of the main Cricut Maker features is that it can type in the same way as it cuts with markers. That implies if you have not-so-great writing, but you still want to create a homemade Mother's Day card without first taking a Scripting lesson, you still can bring off that cute handwritten font.

- Cricut offers a wide selection of colorful pens and markers, and all you have to do is put them into the pen holder, set up your template in Design Space, and got it set instead of Cut as Draw. You have got yourselves a professional-looking written text for whatever project you would like within minutes.

- Design Space has registered brands!

o For all your upcoming projects, this is just a fantastic incentive. You can still cut or sketch your kids' favorite characters, aside from all the fun models and premade projects available in the Design Room. From Star Wars to Wonder to Disney and so many more, you will deck out your kid's wardrobe, bedroom, and school supplies in their beloved TV BFFs.

- The first plan can collapse.

o The slightest suggestion and hope you recall the main takeaway, is that Cricut Creator is not just an instrument. That is like an encounter. There is going to be loads of mistakes. Hiccups could be present. So, there will be occasions that you trash the whole idea and start anew. But if you begin tiny and work up, the stuff you will make would amaze you.

## 2.12 Basic Cricut Terminology

There is a dictionary of Cricut for the basic Cricut terminologies, but here are somethings that you need to know the most:

- **HTV** – Heat Transfer Vinyl (and iron on).

- **631** – Removable vinyl (Indoor, primarily used for window cling, stencils, and temporary wall designs)

- **651** – Permanent vinyl (weatherproof and outdoor).

- **Weeding** – weeding mans to remove the extra vinyl from the cut-out design.

- **Mirror** – This is something you are doing to make sure all the iron-on creations turn out correctly! You do not have to mirror just iron-on projects for regular vinyl designs. At first, you will possibly ignore to mirror a few designs, but as you understand that vinyl is pricey, you would not keep forgetting.

- **Weld** – When you bring together the cursive or script letters and need them to be one word, welding is essential to use. Move the letters next to each other so that they touch, then press "Weld" and they will turn into one piece together! Some wise words for you: After you have completed a project, welding cannot be reversed.

- **Attach** – As the fonts and images are on mat before carving, this retains them such that they do not cut both separately. You can be undone at any time.

- **Group-**This groups items together such that you can track them more quickly.

# Chapter 3: The Design Space

## 3.1 What is Design Space

Imagine that Pinterest had a kid with a mysterious website and that did all the crafting for you effectively. Well, that is Design Space. The application you will use to plan and cut your Cricut projects is the Cricut Design Space. You would need to download and install Cricut Design Space when you set up your Cricut device. Design Space, with its free and easy-to-learn design program, comes with all Cricut machines. It is cloud-based, so from any laptop, you can access your data at any time. Start on your computer, operate it on your mobile, and even work offline, all without breaking your stride. You have the choice of organizing a plan from scratch or choosing from hundreds and thousands of ready-to-make designs. Place the material on a mat, load it in the Cricut, and click the Go button. The Cricut does the rest. Cricut Design Room is the key software that you will use for everything, including uploading pre-made designs, making your own designs, and submitting the Cricut designs so that they can be cut. It will become your best friend and the secret to your imagination.

With Cricut Design Space, there is certainly a learning

process, but once you really start utilizing the software and begin cutting designs, you will get it in no time. On Cricut Design Space, there are also loads of great details and tutorials. To bring the best out of your machine, make sure you benefit from the useful articles they provide. Design Space is a user-friendly and incredibly easy-to-learn software design program and digital resource library that is compatible with various devices such as Windows, Android, iOS, and Mac. Cricut Access is the optional Design Space subscription element that enables you to access additional pre-designed projects (You absolutely can use one without the other). A number of formats, including your jpeg and SVG files and fonts, can also be uploaded.

## 3.2 Installing and uninstalling the design app

- Installing

o Open any internet browser that you have on your computer and go to design.cricut.com.

o Click Download. The screen will change during the download. This happens a little differently in every browser.

o When the download finishes, double-click the file from your browser or in your downloads folder.

o In case a window opens asking if you trust the application, select yes.

o A setup window opens and displays installation progress.

o Use your Cricut ID and password to sign in.

o A Design Space icon will be automatically added to your desktop screen. Right-click on that icon and then choose 'Pin to Taskbar' option or you can drag the icon to the Taskbar as well, to pin the shortcut within an easy reach.

o Now you can enjoy using Design Space for Desktop.

o For sharing feedback, you can use the Feedback tab at the bottom of the Design Space menu.

• Some things to know:

o Your sign in information is remembered by Design Space. You would not have to sign in every time you open Design space unless you have signed out the last time.

o The app does not save automatically. You have to save your projects frequently as you design and also before you close the application.

• Uninstalling

o You have to ensure that Design Space for Desktop is

closed. it will not uninstall properly if the application is not closed.

- o  Now, select the 'Start' icon in the lower left corner of your screen and search for Programs. Select the option 'Add or remove programs. Apps & features window will open.

- o  Use the 'search' field to search "Cricut." Select your Cricut Design Space from the list that appears and then select the 'Uninstall' button.

- o  A confirmation will be required. Confirm that you want to uninstall the Cricut Design Space.

- o  Your system will finish the uninstallation. If prompted, try restarting your computer.

## 3.3 How to use design Space

With the aid of its 900 Plus Simple Video Guides, this app is targeted at the beginner to improve to "Expert." A perfect way to enjoy your Cricut is to use the Cricut Design Space App, access your photos, be ready to cut designs, and best of all, you do not need the Internet for using it.

You can find this app very simple to use if you are already experienced with the Desktop edition of Cricut Design

Space. Only plunge in, press, explore, do not get scared, do not blow up your phone or iPad! A sheet of paper guiding you on how to download and install Cricut Design Space will be included in the box with your brand new Cricut machine.

Just in case you are not able to find it, you can visit **https://design.cricut.com/setup** on whatever device (computer, laptop, tablet, or phone) you are using to create projects with your Cricut. This provided link will take you through the set-up procedure, step by step and teach you how to plug in and control your machine if you have not already done so.

Firstly, you have to make sure that your computer, phone, or tablet has Bluetooth activated. You will usually find the Bluetooth option under 'Setup' based on the type of model that you are using. You have to make sure it is on. Switch on your Cricut, if you have not already, by momentarily keeping down its power button, which is on the right side of your machine. Look for your machine to show up in the list of devices while your computer's or phone's Bluetooth settings are open. Tap on it when you see it and want to connect. You can be asked at this stage to enter a passcode: if so, use 0000.

If, for whatever cause, you cannot get Bluetooth to function or just do not have it on your system, simply use the provided USB cable to link your machine and the Cricut.

Your machine and Cricut will be connected and are ready to use. Everything that needs to be achieved now is to begin designing.  What's unique about the Design Space is that it is designed especially for beginners and offers step-by-step guidelines on how each project should be begun and finished. It is so convenient to use that it is probably a little limiting for more advanced people, but there is no need to think about it until later.

When you sign in to your Cricut Design Space profile and choose to open or update a new project, you can do that from a window named Canvas.

In Cricut Design Space, the Canvas Region is where you do all the edits until your designs are cut.

There are too many keys, options, and stuff to do that could make you feel confused.

So, in this section, you are about to discover what every icon is for in the field of Canvas. Let's split the canvas into four regions and four colors to maintain it in order and simple to grasp.

- Upper Yellow Panel. This is the Editing Area

The top panel is for the editing and organizing objects on the canvas region in the Design Space Canvas area. You can select what sort of font you would want to use from this panel; you can adjust sizes, match styles, and more!

This panel is classified into two more sub-panels. The first one helps your tasks to be saved, named, and eventually cut. And the second panel will enable you to monitor the canvas region and edit items.

o Sub-panel #1 Name and Cut the Project

This sub-panel lets you navigate your projects, profile from the Canvas, and even send your finished projects to be cut.

o Subpanel 2- Editing Menu

It is very helpful to arrange, edit, and organize images and fonts in the Canvas Region.

- Blue Left Panel. This is the Insert Area

You will modify all the designs with the top panel (described earlier in this section).

But where do they come from? They all come from the Left Panel of the Cricut Design Room.

This panel is more about inserting images, shapes, ready to

cut projects, and much more. You are going to insert all the things from here that you are going to cut.

There are seven choices for this panel:

o New: in the canvas field, to create and replace a new project.

o Templates: this makes it easier for you to provide a reference about the sorts of items you are going to cut. Let's just assume that you want to iron a onesie on vinyl. You will plan and see how the design would appear when you pick the template.

o Projects: Insert ready to cut Cricut Access projects.

o Images: To make a project, pick images from Cricut Access and cartridges.

o Text: To add text to your canvas area, click text.

o Shapes: On the canvas, for adding all sorts of shapes.

o Uploads: Upload the cut files and images to the Design Space.

o On this panel, you need to acknowledge something essential; Cricut fonts, projects ready to cut, and Cricut images cost money unless you have Cricut Access. If you need them, you are going to have to pay before cutting your project.

- Right, Purple Panel. This is the Layers Panel

To set you up for progress and before the clarification to you what every symbol is all about on the Layers Screen, lets send you a little insight into what a layer is.

Layers define every single feature or pattern that is on the canvas region.

Think about it as clothing; you have several layers that make up your outfit when you get ready, and your outfit can be primary or complicated based on the day or time of year.

So, the fabrics will be underwear, skirts, tops, coats, socks, boots, gloves, etc., on a cold day, but you would just have one sheet for a day at the beach, a swimsuit!

The same applies to a design; you will have various styles of layers that would make up your whole layout, depending on the scope of the project you are working on.

Let's imagine, for now, that you are making a Christmas Card.

What's this card going to have?

Maybe a text that says Happy Christmas, the card itself, a flower, maybe an envelope, too?

The argument is that there are layers of all the little designs and components that are part of that project.

Few layers may be modified, while other layers cannot be modified, such as JPEG and PNG photos, regardless of the file's design or even the layer itself.

For example, a text layer may be transformed to other layer styles, but you would sacrifice the ability to edit the text if you do that.

You can think more of what you can or cannot do with layers when you move.

- Green Canvas Area

The canvas region is where all your elements and designs are used. It is simple and really intuitive to use!

The canvas region is separated by a line; this is perfect, so you can imagine the cutting mat for any little square you see on the grid. This can help you maximize your area in the end.

When you press on the top panel toggle, you can adjust the dimensions from inches to cm, switch the grid on and off, and then choose Settings. A window with all options will pop up.

The selection is blue if you pick one or more layers, and you may change it from any of the four corners.

The "red x" is for the layers to be deleted. The upper right corner helps you to rotate the pic.

When you decrease or increase your layer's size, the lower right button of the pick, "the small lock," holds the size proportional. You are also going to get various amounts by tapping on it.

Lastly, you may do this by clicking the + and - signs on the lower-left corner of your canvas if you choose to see on a greater or smaller scale (without altering the actual size of the designs).

## 3.4 Using the Design Space app

The application is cloud-based, meaning you can view your templates and profiles with every platform that has the app.

And it is suitable for individuals who keep traveling or for others who want to use their Cricut account when they do not have access to an internet connection.

In order to create something while being offline, just make sure you save all fonts and images you need to use offline. Tap the save icon and click 'save as' to save offline usage tasks, then save to your computer. Only bring down the Categories screen and click 'My Projects on this iPad' (or on whatever device you are using at the moment). Anytime you want to reach your projects when you are offline and launch it from there.

The Cricut Design Space Canvas Region is where all the fun takes place before your designs are cut. Design Space would be where you touch up your creations and arrange them. Not only can you use and upload your fonts and photos in this room, but Cricut's premium images and fonts can also be accessed by individual transactions, Cartridges, and Cricut Access. You can find the hundreds of various creations accessible in the app for you to experience while you are in online mode, as well as the ability to build designs completely from scratch utilizing the 'new canvas' feature.

Some cool features of Design Space are:

- You may fully personalize the learning process and make it easier to replay lessons taken in the past.

- Maintain your own collection of notes for any video so that it can be conveniently accessed when a refresher is required.

- You can make videos your favorite.

- Offer every video a rating.

- Drag & drop video to put it wherever you want it within its category.

- Adjust the category of videos.

- Note, subtitle or title search.

- Filter by group, favorites, or rating.

- Viewing Recent History.

## 3.5 Is there any difference between the Design Space App for iPhone and iPad?

Luckily, there is not a major difference between the two options for us. Can you imagine trying to understand and learn two separate applications?

Space management is the only minor difference between the iPhone Application and the iPad application.

On the top panel offered on the iPad, you can still see the names first, although, on the tablet, you can also see a rectangle split into three equal sections. They both reflect the same thing, though.

Something to bear in mind also is that the menus are really

long most of the time when you click on something, so you will have to slide them to the right and left with the handset to see all the choices, even with the iPad.

Also, since there is limited space on phones, the layers button will be disabled several times on your screen when you tap on other functions. You can keep the Layers button visible all the time on your iPad.

## 3.6 Differences between the Cricut Designs Space App and Desktop

While you can do almost everything you can think of, on the Design Space App. The desktop interface does have several other features.

Of course, you do not want to scramble to locate some features on the app to smash your brain, so let's mention them for you:

- **Select All:** This button allows user to select all the elements and layers he/she has on the canvas area.

- **Curve Text:** This feature allows user to curve text. This can only be found and used in the desktop version of Design Space.

- **Advanced (Ungroup to layers and lines):** The Design

- Space App would not allow users to ungroup fonts to lines, when they have a paragraph, or in layers when they have a Multi-Layer font. Users can only do this to letters.

- **Patterns:** unfortunately, Users can only use and upload the patterns on the desktop version of Design Space.

- **Templates:** Templates are an amazing way for users to visualize where their designs will go. This feature is available on the desktop version of Design Space only.

**SnapMat:** This cool feature is only found in app and the desktop version does not have it. This feature allows users to choose the exact location on their mat, where they want their Cricut to cut.

## 3.6 Why Design Space was shifted from a website to Desktop App?

More than seven months ago, the desktop version of this software was released. You might have noticed reminders to update it, and you might even have it on your device. When it is linked to the internet, there are absolutely no discrepancies between the desktop app and the web app. You only enter Cricut Design Space through your device instead of a website.

- Auto updates (this in itself makes it all worth it!) that do not need you to upgrade your plugin.

- Faster connections between your Cricut and your computer.

- Using the Design Space app is just like using the website, plus the internet quality usually does not interfere (not sure about this one; see below)

- Updated Capabilities for searching

## 3.7 Working Offline with Cricut Design Space

For those crafters who operate on the fly and who are never too sure which pictures and fonts they are going to want, it is hard for them to make sure that they have them saved before they go offline.

That being said, the usage of Design Space offline is feasible. Here are several drawbacks to operating offline in Design Space until you get into saving designs, photos, and fonts for offline use:

When offline, you will not be able to upload your own files to Design Space.

Templates cannot be used when offline.

Only projects, photos, and fonts that you saved before going offline would be available to you.

You get to have an internet connection to save things for offline use. Before moving offline, you need to be online.

For offline cutting, there are two ways that can save a whole project.

- The first one is when your idea is finalized. Plan a project and press the Save button in the upper right corner. You can give your project a tag, and you will determine whether you want to save it for offline usage on the next screen:

- If you have a previously saved project, in the upper right, go to 'My Projects,' click on the project and click "Save for Offline." The next time you are in Design Space, even without the internet, you will be able to use it.

So far in the app, saving a picture for offline usage has been fascinating. You would notice that every picture you place on the canvas in the app so would be saved immediately as an image you can use offline.

To save a picture that you want to use offline, check for an image in the Cricut Image Library (on the left side of your canvas, press Images), pick an image, and then click Save at the bottom left. For offline usage, this will save your image.

Make a text box using the Text function on the left side of the Canvas to save the Cricut font for offline use. Use the filter in the dropdown to choose only Cricut fonts. You may pick a font you like to save offline from here. To the right, there would be a "download" tab. Click it, and you can get your font saved for offline usage.

Note: without saving your device fonts for offline use, you can still use them offline. There is no need to save them since they already exist on your device.

# Chapter 4: Cricut Access

## 4.1 What is Cricut Access

Cricut Access is a paid subscription that allows you immediate access to an incredible and vast library full of over 90,000 pictures, thousands of fonts, and designs ready to be cut. On products, templates, and shipping, you will even get discounts. It is necessary to remember that these pictures are not yours. Only when you have subscribed to a Cricut Access package, then you have access to them. You would not be allowed to use them for free when that is over.

## 4.2 Do you need it?

Cricut Access is genuinely the best way to go if you possess a Cricut Maker or Cricut Explore Air. All the money you have invested in a fantastic gadget, so you would better use it. Do not let it stay in the corner and transform it into an accessory for a decorative rack. Put your Cricut to work. It will amaze you, and you will be addicted within hours. You would come up with every justification under the sun for using your laptop as soon as you get the membership for Cricut Access. You are going to discover images you never imagined existed, and you are going to have fun utilizing them in imaginative ways.

It is worth it if Cricut Access motivates you to use the machine more frequently, if you do not know how to explain or create your own designs, and if you do not want to browse online for free projects.

Do you make crafts and projects of your own? If yes, you do not need Cricut Access then.

Are you able to search the Internet for suggestions and free projects? You do not need Cricut Access if you say yes to that.

You do not require Cricut Access to cut things. For you to choose, there are still other options. There is something you really need to trade-off though, that is TIME!

It will take a while to plan and look for the ideal project. There are still details you need to touch up when you search a project online and additional measures for you to make sure you cut it the correct way. However, all the second thoughts almost vanish when you are using the Cricut Access photos and cut projects. No wonder you just have to click MAKE IT and obey the directions for cutting.

If it is going to make your life simpler to have Cricut Access and just appreciate the enjoyable part of cutting and getting your project together, then the subscription is worth every penny! The membership will add up because, on top of your bills, it is an extra expense. et once you think about it, you will find you are investing $10 on too many silly things already, so why not this.? They still have outstanding discounts for members of Cricut Access if you intend to order more products, machines, and accessories from cricut.com. Therefore, if the sales are high enough as you claim the discount, Cricut Access will be eligible theoretically.

## 4.3 Is it worth it?

Here are some reasons why Cricut Access is worth buying and will surely worth each penny of yours:

- You will get access to 100,000+ images for a quite low price. And images are added on a weekly basis.

- You will get access to 400 fonts, which includes Writing fonts as well.

- If you buy any image or font from the Design Space App, an Access subscription will pay very quickly for itself.

- Quick member support. It is twice as fast. Also, you get priority support if you have Cricut Access over those who do not have Access.

- You get 10% saving on all the product purchases from cricut.com which includes accessories, machines, materials, and much more.

- You also get 10% savings on the premium licensed images, fonts, and ready-to-make projects from some brands.

- There are also exclusive discounts on products, like the Cricut Joy Bundle the March 2020 Mystery Box.

- Exclusive product offers for Access members.

- If you have a craft business, then you get a tax deduction.

- You can now craft faster because you no longer have to buy or search for free projects or make it yourself.

## 4.4 Difference between Cricut Design Space and Cricut Access

Cricut Access is an exclusive membership package that offers benefits for free and approved designs at a reduced price, such as access to Cricut fonts, images, and projects. The free application that you use to make or upload templates and cut them on your Cricut is Cricut Design

Space. The free Cricut Design Space app must be downloaded and used by all Cricut Explore family, Cricut Maker, and Cricut Joy users. The contrast between Cricut Design Space and Cricut Access is that the Design Space is a free program where you import, edit, and eventually submit your designs to be cut to your Cricut Machine. And the Cricut Access is a paid subscription full of designs that can be used inside the Cricut Design Space, these designs can be images, fonts, and ready to cut projects as well.

Even if you do not have a Cricut Access subscription, all the graphics they provide inside the Cricut Design Space can be used. When you submit your idea to be cut, though, you may need to pay for such digital data. When anything costs cash or not, it is always very obvious. But if you do not want to pay, or do not have connections to Cricut, remain out of the projects.

You can upload your own templates, use your own fonts, and even make minimal designs created of typical shapes, including squares, triangles, hearts, etc., with Cricut Design Space and for free.

## 4.5 Cricut Access plans

You ought to have an understanding by now whether the Cricut Access is a decent match for you or not. Right?

Now let's clarify what plans are available, what these plans have in common, and how they vary from each other.

All the Cricut Access plans include access to the following:

- Unlimited use of more than 50.000 graphics, images, and ready-to-cut projects.

- Unlimited use of more than 400 fonts.

- Upto 10% Savings on all the tangible products and goods purchased from cricut's website.

- Upto 10% Savings on cartridges, images, ready-to-cut projects, fonts from various brands like Sesame Street, Disney, Hello Kitty, etc.

- Priority Member Care Line which provides 50% less waiting time.

Now let's compare the names and features of each plan:

- The perfect starter plan

If you are only testing the waters and want to know if Cricut Access makes sense to you, this is the best plan. And even if it does not work well for you, remember, you can cancel at any moment. This plan is charged on a monthly basis, which costs $9.99.

- Annual Plan

This plan has the same advantages as the Perfect Starter Plan. It is charged annually, so instead of $9.99, you have to pay $7.99 per month. Here you sign a one-year agreement to pay $95.88 upfront.

- Premium Plan

As well as all of the advantages described above. It even offers you the highest benefit: further discounts. On licensed graphics, fonts, and ready-to-make and cut designs, up to 50 percent. When you order for more than $50, you also get Free Economy Shipping (this does not involve products such as Disney, Hello Kitty, Sesame Street, and other major brands). You have to pay $119.88 upfront annually. (That will be $9.99 a month).

## 4.6 Which membership should you choose?

| Fonts membership | Standard membership | Premium membership |
|---|---|---|
| Starting at | Starting at | Just |
| $4.99/mo | $7.99/mo | $9.99/mo |
| billed annually. Or $6.99/mo billed monthly. | billed annually. Or $9.99/mo billed monthly. | billed annually. |
| **The perfect starter membership** | **Big-time benefits** | **The best value** |
| √ Unlimited access to over 400 beautiful fonts | √ Unlimited access to over 400 beautiful fonts | √ Unlimited access to over 400 beautiful fonts |
| √ Priority Member Care line option | √ Unlimited use of over 30,000 covet-worthy, cut-ready premium Cricut images, including exclusive designs | √ Unlimited use of over 30,000 covet-worthy, cut-ready premium Cricut images, including exclusive designs |
| | √ 10% savings on licensed fonts, images, and ready-to-make projects | √ 10% savings on licensed fonts, images, and ready-to-make projects |
| | √ 10% savings on all product purchases on cricut.com, including machines, accessories, materials, and more' | √ 10% savings on all product purchases on cricut.com, including machines, accessories, materials, and more' |
| | √ Priority Member Care line option | √ Up to 50% savings on designer fonts, images, and ready-to-make projects' |
| | | √ Free economy shipping on orders over $50 |
| | | √ Priority Member Care line option |

Each plan has added benefits, as you can see in the above table. It is solely your choice to determine which one suits your needs. You can pick depending on your crafting requirements, but everyone loves the 10 percent discounts on all product transactions on cricut.com, and 10 percent savings on Regular and Premium membership certified fonts, photos, and ready-to-make projects! Plus, there is a Priority Member Care telephone line for every plan you choose that takes you up in the list, and so, it gets your questions answered quickly!

For Cricut Access, Fonts are the first subscription. Cricut provides more than 400 fonts, and when paid annually or $6.99 per month if charged monthly, this monthly subscription is as little as $4.99.

The Cricut Access Standard is the next plan. You will be able to browse more than 400 fonts and more than 30,000 images and cut files with this subscription. Besides, this package gives a 10 percent discount on product purchases with certain exclusions, as well as on fonts and images that are not included in the subscription.

It is also possible to bill this subscription monthly or yearly. Standard memberships commence monthly at $7.99 or yearly at $9.99 per month. On this package, yearly subscribers save $24!

The Cricut Access Premium is the final plan (and the best of all plans). The Premium membership is, indeed, Premium! This covers all images, all fonts but still has a half-off discount for texts and images that were not included in the subscription. (Exclusions are there)

And there is more, on cricut.com, Cricut Access - Premium members even get free Economy delivery on purchases above $50. This plan of membership provides the most access and is the best offer overall. For just under $120, this is an annual plan.

Auto-renewal of Cricut Access subscriptions is provided. At https://cricut.com/customer/account, you can manage this auto-renewal. If you have subscribed to access through your android or iOS app, iTunes or Google Play will allow you to change or cancel your subscription.

## 4.7 Steps to purchase Cricut Access

You may purchase Cricut Access plans via Cricut.com, Cricut Design Space on a desktop or mobile device (Android or iOS), or via the Cricut Joy app (iOS). Make sure they are fully up to date in order to use this option through your mobile apps. You will get some perks, such as discounts on approved images, fonts, and actual products, based on the package you have.

Note: Availability of Cricut Access plans may vary based on your country and platform.

To purchase Cricut Access plan, follow these steps.

- First Sign-in to your Design Space.

- Click the Design Space menu (☰) and select **Cricut Access**.

- Depending upon your trial eligibility:

- In case you are eligible for the free trial, the opportunity to launch your trial will be given to you. Click 'Start My Trial'.

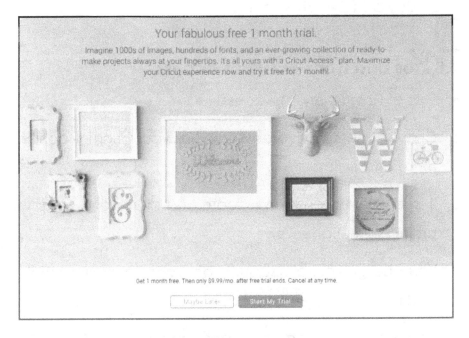

- You can see an offer for purchasing either the Monthly or Yearly plan of Cricut Access if you have had a free trial already.

- Enter and review your account details, then click Confirm/Continue. Enter your password, if asked, to approve your purchase.

  Note: The postal code or ZIP code field will be shown when you enter your card number.

  - Your Cricut Access tier will be activated immediately and is accessible on all software platforms for Cricut Joy and Design Space.

## 4.8 Pros and Cons of Cricut Access

- Pros of Having Cricut Access

o Cricut Access motivates you to use your Cricut Machine more often.

o It is so easy for anyone to learn and for making elegant projects simultaneously.

o You also get extra discounts on accessories, materials, and machines from cricut.com.

o You do not need any past experience to make something incredible.

o You can find almost everything you want for any affair, at any time of the year.

- o  If you obey the guidance, be confident that the fonts and templates that you have got access to will function.

- • Cons of Having Cricut Access

- o  It is a recurring investment. You would not have unrestricted access to all the previews used with fonts or icons when you quit paying.

- o  You can use them in Cricut Design Space only. Forget to use other applications, including Inkspace or Adobe Illustrator, to combine certain fonts and pictures.

## 4.9 Are there any other alternative Options for Cricut Access?

You require Cricut Design Space in order for you to cut your designs. However, as described earlier in this book, you may have your own files cut and upload them.

There is a question. Where will these files be found?

Every week, Cricut Design Space provides Free Cuts, so take advantage of the chance.

There are many bloggers that enjoy Cricut and have tons of fun downloadable projects and tutorials for you. On Pinterest and Google, you can find lots of files and tutorials. You can also purchase them from websites like TheHungryJpeg, Creative Market, and Etsy, which have many options to consider for you. They can be designed and made as well. It takes time and dedication, it is like discovering a whole new skill, and well, this is what the best option is. Lastly, you can have a paid software such as Illustrator or get open-source software such as Inkscape.

## 4.10 How to find its content.

The Cricut Access icon flags fonts, images, patterns, and also some Ready-to-Make projects that are included in Cricut Access (this icon appears whether Cricut Access is active on your Design Space account or not). Please follow the steps below to find the fonts, images, patterns, and ready-to-make projects that are included in Cricut Access:

First, Sign-in to your Design Space at **design.cricut.com**, then click at '**New Project**'.

- For ready-to-make Projects

- From the left side panel, click 'Projects'.

- A drop-down menu will appear. Click Cricut Access.

- For Images

- At left, on the canvas, in design panel, click 'Images'.

- Click 'Browse All Images' near 'Search' field.

- Click the 'Cricut Access' box. This page will reload and now, it will show only the Cricut Access images.

Note: You may also select the Image Sets under the Highlighted Categories and then apply the filter 'Cricut Access' in order to see the Cricut Access image sets. You can also select some additional filters or enter any search term in order to narrow down the search. Then select 'Clear-All' in order to clear all the applied filters.

- For Fonts

- From the left of the canvas, select 'Text' from the design panel.

- At the top, 'Text Edit bar' will appear on the screen.

- Now, from the left of the bar, click 'Fonts' drop-down menu, in order to view the fonts' list.

- The fonts included in Cricut Access will flag with a Cricut Access icon

Note: In case you have a Cricut Access plan activated, it will not show you price next to the fonts.

# Chapter 5: How to start?

## 5.1 How much does it cost to get started?

As you might have expected, the cost of operating your Cricut businesses may differ based on what crafts products you want to produce and sell using your Cricut machine. This section will discuss the basic materials you need to sell different crafts, products, and Cricut projects.

Please note that according to where you buy your materials from, your prices can vary. Note that you will need additional materials for your crafts and products to be packed and shipped. The estimates for the calculation do not include taxes or delivering your materials to you. These calculations also presume that you have a Cricut machine, Cricut mats, and Cricut basic toolset.

You might be wondering if you are going to use your Cricut machine enough to justify the price. So, yes, you do. But merely saying that is probably not a great response, so here are some statistics.

You can purchase Cricut Explore Air 2 for $229.999 right now. That will be around $20 a month if you have savings of a year. If you just chose to have lunch at home once in a week and save $5 per week, you would have an additional $20 for the machine. It is an investment, but it is worthwhile.

You would use Cricut sufficiently to justify your investment, if:

- You enjoy creating unique projects and you make your own designs

Have you drawn any hand-lettered illustrations that you like to attach to a notebook? Upload a picture of your own and cut out the vinyl. Or have you drawn a brilliant cartoon and would like to create a shirt out of that? Upload it on Design Space and cut out in the Cricut Iron-on.

- You have fun customizing things

Do you enjoy creating special gifts and surprises for your loved ones? Using Cricut to add your special touch to greeting cards, presents, and so much more is fun. You really cannot stop once you begin doing so.

Do you enjoy sorting stuff and labeling them?

Will you enjoy sitting in your pantry with pretty labels? Are your drawers all arranged into various items? The opportunities on what you can mark and arrange are infinite. Enjoy making custom home decor

Create your own designs, stencils, personalize your furniture with foil or vinyl designs, make customized fabrics, pillows, etc.

## 5.2 How to make your first Cricut Project?

Start doing something is the best way to understand it. Get the machine out of the package, plug it in, and use a Bluetooth connection or a cable to connect to your mobile, computer, or tablet.

On your tablet, mobile, or computer (go to cricut.com/setup), open Cricut Design Space. You would be guided to move through a couple of steps for setting up your account and then registering the Cricut machine. This would only take you 10 minutes.

You are ready to create something new. You have the option to create your own template to cut OR make something from the "Make it Now" that are projects meant to be created from start to the end. You should save your favorite ideas to build later!

The available membership of Cricut Access (less than $10 a month) would grant you access to a wide range of free projects and additional affordable projects that you will retain after purchase.

If different resources are needed for a project, you will be instructed to prepare each mat with the correct material and adjust blades for various forms of cuts, such as scoring or cutting.

## 5.3 Necessary Supplies

- FOR CRAFT SPACE

  Are you ready for starting set up of your craft space? Here is a list of things you must have:

- A desk, countertop, or a desk with a comfortable chair. Extra credit if there are wheels on your chair.

- Some space for storing your things. This machine is not massive, but neither is it small, so do not expect to keep it on a shelf that is either very high or very low. The preferred place to store it is on a rolling cart, but you can also put it somewhere that is easy to reach with minimum effort.

- Good lighting is essential. This because after you complete your video lessons and learn more about weeding, you will know that you need the finest set of glasses and some super bright lights. The average light on your ceiling would not be enough. In your workspace, go for LED lights.

- Boxes or containers. You might have begun by grabbing a package, or maybe you are only purchasing materials project by project. Whatever path you pursue, you can end up with lots of stuff to store. To differentiate your equipment and materials, go for containers with transparent lids, and make sure to use your Cricut to mark your boxes so that it remains clean and tidy.
- FOR PROJECTS:

There are things you need for every of the Cricut tasks you may speak about. It would be essential to have a Cricut machine, Cricut basic toolset, and a Cricut mat for every Cricut business project. Cricut comes with a Cricut mat when you first purchase it, and certain Cricut packages come with the fundamental toolset, vinyl, mats, and more.

  o Heat transfer vinyl projects or T-shirts.

Cost: The costs for vinyl heat transfer projects vary considerably. It would not cost you more than $10 to get most of the tote bags, t-shirts, beauty bags, etc.

T-shirts or some other supplies such as tote bag, cloth or canvas, onesie, makeup bag, apron, kitchen towel, koozie, pillowcase, potholder, etc.

Heat press, Cricut EasyPress Mat, heat transfer vinyl Iron,

Cricut EasyPress. parchment paper, Teflon sheet, Towel.

- o Wood Signs

Cost: The price for projects with wood signs differs based on the kind of wood sign you choose to sell. You may sell square wood signs (most commonly used for wedding signs), circular wood signs, or rectangular signs (often used for door signs of homes). With less than $20, you will get much of the wood.

Wood, stain brush, wood stain, paint, paint brush, vinyl

- o Welcome Door Mat

Cost: You can get plain door mats in less than $15.

Welcome mat, spray paint, paint, paint brush, masking tape, painter's tape, 651 Vinyl.

- o Mugs or Tumblers

Cost: Tumblers are available just about everywhere, and for branded tumblers such as Yeti, the cost of the tumblers ranges from $10 and up to $50+.

Tumbler, mug, transfer tape, 651 Vinyl.

- o Wine Glass

Cost: Just about everywhere, from Walmart,

Amazon, Target, etc., you can buy wine glasses. You can get four glasses in a package at Walmart for around $20.

Wine Glass, transfer tape, 651 Vinyl or etching cream,

- Leather Hair Bows

Cost: You can get these for less than $65, 24 faux leather packs, $12 for a standard hot glue gun, and $8 for a typical hair clip.

Hot glue gun, faux leather, hair clip

- Keychains

Cost: In less than $30, you will get these. Including five key chains, one "6 x 100" transfer tape roll, and One "12 x 24" glitter vinyl sheet.

Key chain, transfer tape, 651 Vinyl

- Cake or Cupcake Toppers

Cost: It costs less than $20, based on one box of skewers or toothpicks and one pack of cardstock.

Cardstock, wood skewers or toothpicks.

- Paper Crafts

Cost: It costs less than $40, based on one glue gun and three packs of cardstock.

Cardstock, hot glue gun, glue stick, tape.

Examples include gift tags, greeting cards, envelopes, confetti, paper flowers.

- o Stickers

Cost: It costs less than $15 excluding the printer.

Printer, sticker paper, ink.

## 5.4 Decide your Craft Niche

One of the biggest mistakes you can make is merely continuing to do whatever people want you to do. Here a tumbler, there a home decor tag, then birthday t-shirts. You are probably going to end up with smaller margins, lost products, and a disappointed audience.

Instead, narrow down the product range to one or two products or trends, and then prove yourself. It is recommend choosing something at the intersection between what you love to produce and what is profitable. You want to love what you make, and you want that product worth your time and money.

Consider "added value" as you want to determine what products to create and sell from your Cricut. These may involve all enhancements to your product. You may charge a premium for your goods this way.

For example, several individuals create home decor signs. Maybe adding hand-painted glitter or paper succulents is your "niche."

If you create tumblers, they could be directly targeted to instructors and come with a gift card. Your shop could be full of cute items, particularly for premature infants. You should spend extra if you are one of the few people doing that. It also helps in focusing your advertisements quickly.

Note: the bigger the project, the more challenging and more costly it will be to ship. For the local craft fair, you should save those gigantic home decor signs.

## 5.5 Buy Materials in bulk

You can purchase your materials and supplies in bulk if you have nailed your niche. If you buy in bulk, you can get more vinyl or tumblers or mugs at a lower cost. It is much harder to buy in bulk if you are only making "one off" products.

For example, if you are designing vacation t-shirts, you can buy them in bulk to reduce expenses instead of buying the usual rolls of iron-on vinyl from a store.

## 5.6 Slowly invest in your business

You do not want to suddenly dump all your money in your business, of course. Begin simple and develop friendships and consumers who enjoy the product with a loyal following. Ask them for feedback. If you deliver a beautiful, value-added product, high quality, they will continue to suggest you to their mates. You are on to it once they start shopping, and you start to receive revenue from people outside your circle.

This is a good signal that the idea has a viable demand!

Then start putting aside a small sum of your earnings to bring your business into progress. It would help if you gradually increase the business, whether that is another tumbler turner, second EasyPress, or Facebook ads.

## 5.7 Do not sell your Projects too cheap

When there are individuals seen selling their Cricut goods for crazy cheap online and at art fairs, it is always upsetting. These sellers should be told that they do not really respect their own ability or time!

So, promise yourself, you are going to pay for what your project is worth! Do not sell low on yourself. If you are hardly making money (or even worse, wasting money!), you can stress out easily.

Bear one thing in mind: reduced rates do not always mean higher profits. If you are underpriced, customers may believe you are offering a sub-quality commodity. Alternatively, if you charge higher, they will always assume that you are offering premium quality goods.

## 5.8 Do Calculate your Costs

Pricing is indeed challenging! You want to charge sufficiently to earn sales with your Cricut, but not so high that your product would not sell. In order to reach the price mark that makes sense, you can need to play around with the pricing, but here are some useful instructions:

Start by evaluating your expenditures. And by this, it means all the expenditures.

Let's presume you are creating hand-painted, stenciled Christmas signs. You are going to need to pay for:

- The Cricut mat. use one Cricut mat again and again, and make hashmarks, until it becomes unusable. This will let you know that how many stencils you are able to cut with one Cricut mat.

- Stencil blank. Use hashmark method as stated above.

- Wood craft frame

- Masking tape. Note how much you need to use for one sign.

- Craft paint. Draw a mark on the bottle that shows how much you use for one sign.

- Sponge stippler brushes. Do keep a track of the number of signs you can make before they start tearing and wear out.

- Paint brush for touching up.

- Cricut blade. You must keep a track of how long it works and when you need to replace it.

Sum that up, and then include your TIME. Calculate a price per hour you like to make and apply it to the cost of supply. Generally speaking, the sale price would be anywhere from 2-4 times your supply rate.

In order to see if you are in the correct ballpark, you should even search other distributors, but note that cheaper does not necessarily mean better revenue.

## 5.9 Check Sales Tax and Shipping costs

To see whether you need to raise or remit sales tax, search your localities. Also, you will want to put aside a part of your tax profit. This is one place you ought to consult with an accountant.

You will have to do some analysis on the safest and least costly way to ship the goods if you are selling internationally. You may calculate the shipping cost within your price, but what is preferred is that you mention it separately. People are accustomed to paying for delivery from smaller sellers, along with the pace of today's world.

You should still provide limited-time free delivery as a value add at particular occasions of the year, such as Black Friday or the business's anniversary if it fits your pricing module.

## 5.10 How to sell cricut projects

While selling crafts, as it points out, the smaller the project, the more successful it ends up becoming. Smaller implies that there is less material to create the item and less weight while shipping, which means 'better profit.'

So, a person's primary concern in designing a Cricut

business plan is the cost of supplies, shipping requirements and general size time and commitment from beginning to end (since time is precious!), and popularity.

- **Cost of Materials** – Production costs typically fold into pricing. However, operating costs are something you might want to remember. Many citizens have to bring resources first to purchase supplies. There will be some surplus materials and scraps for bulk sales. It would help if you still attempt to acquire as much product as you may require, but that is never optimized correctly.

- **Shipping** – There have been several claims that while delivery is easy, customers only purchase more. This is typically achievable for the vendor by folding the delivery costs into the price of the goods. If you have a premium price value object, everything is good, but if the product's natural price is $5 and delivery costs $50, that really does not make logic to the end customer.

- **Effort** – This is mostly a labor of passion for most crafters to market their items. But when creating crafts for customers takes over your life, it does take away from the pleasure. Do you really want to work for several days and just sell it for $5 if you sell a very complicated vinyl piece? In the world of business, the days you have to miss the family picnic or wait up most of the night since you have a deadline to follow is a bitter truth. It is simply something to take into consideration.

- **Popularity** – It never hurts to make a trend as they come and go. That is the beauty of selling homemade; the supply chain and practices appear to be more flexible such that if the winds shift course, you can pivot. You should turn gears and start thinking about what people want, whether it is new movies and songs, activities, or some other element that sparks a current trend.

## 5.11 Earning with Vinyl Cutter

For business sellers at Cricut, vinyl is the right material. It is pretty cheap, lightweight, and extremely easy to deliver, and also, there are so many items you can create, most significantly.

- **Wall Art**

The options here are infinite. Farmhouse wall decoration is always going high. On Pinterest, there are now more than half million searches monthly for wall art of farmhouses.

- **Customized Decals**

Custom designed stickers are perfect as they apply from events to home decor and so many ultimate uses. It is a difference that the larger stores will not be able to compete with as you provide personalized service.

- **Kids Related Wall Decals**

Decorating relevant to children occurs during the year. There is an everlasting need for decor for babies and teens, from baby showers to birthday parties and even nurseries.

- **Stickers**

Stickers and vinyl decals both are a popular item because of the modification opportunities and their delivery rates (as it is not costly)

- **Wedding Décor**

The demand for weddings is well and alive. It is not a surprise. Back yard weddings are on the rise, according to Pinterest. The quest for them has risen by 441 percent. Everyone manages to save a bit for their wedding. Although individuals have smaller affairs, they cut down on the details. A more personalized touch was needed for small intimate occurrences. The best items for today's wedding are handcrafted items, tailored wedding party gear, and personalized favors.

## 5.12  Earning with Cricut Explorer 2

- **Paper Flowers**

The trend of floral arrangements made of paper is at an all-time peak, much as farmhouse decor, with even more than half-million monthly searches on Pinterest for it. From Mother's Day to celebrations to family weddings and baby showers, they are perfect for all times.

- **Cricut Cake Toppers**

The simplest and most cost-effective items to produce could be cake and cupcake toppers. Parents are still looking at uplifting their game at their child's birthday parties with all kinds of personalized decor and favors. Unicorns are really the rage among children these days.

- **Leather Earrings**

The adorable leather earrings take no exceptional potential to be produced by any graphic design. Just go and get a little free leather swatch from the furniture market and use them to create an initial batch if you only want to measure the water.

## 5.13 Earning with Cricut Maker

The options are now utterly infinite with the top-of-the-line Cricut Machines, such as the Cricut Maker. There are so many things to deal with, from fabric to paper to wood.

- **Felt and Fabric Flowers**

According to Pinterest, searches for Cactus arrangements were up 235 percent. So, get on with this succulent fashion.

- **Wood Projects**

There are more than one million searches monthly for rustic decor on Pinterest. With your Cricut Maker, you can cut wood coincidentally! A sure bet is personalized wood signs.

- **Other Leather and Faux Leather Goods**

With the Cricut Explorer, you can definitely cut leather and faux leather both, but it is undoubtedly simpler with the Rotary blade and knife blade. Some of the more beautiful shiny and decorative faux leathers are very smooth, and with the Rotary blade, you can make it to cut continuously.

## 5.14 Where to sell your Cricut Projects

Here are a few places you might want to sell your amazing Cricut creations so you can make money with your Cricut!

- Through word-of-mouth, locally.

- Any local art and craft fair.

- A pop-up shop near your church, retailer, or school.

- Personal Instagram or Facebook page.

- Facebook or Instagram business page. Or through WhatsApp business.

- Facebook groups. But in this case, you have to make sure your moderator grants you permission.

- You can have your own online shop on:

  o **WooCommerce**

  o **Shopify**

  o **Square Space**

  o **Amazon Handmade Seller Marketplace**

  o **Etsy**

  o **Instagram**

  o **eBay**

# Chapter 6: DIYs with Cricut Machine.

It is too much fun to make designs with Cricut. Through your Cricut Maker and Cricut Explore cutting machines, you can make all types of crafts. There are so many excellent designs of Cricut to consider. You can find a large number of tutorials for tasks here.

## 6.1 Infusible Ink T-shirt Tutorial

Sanitize your hands with soap before you are starting this project and dry them fully.

Cricut Infusible Ink can be extremely susceptible to heat and moisture. Remove the moisture or lotion on your hands. Try wearing any plastic gloves if your palms sweat constantly.

**Supplies:**

- o Standard Grip Mat
- o Cricut EasyPress Mat
- o Cricut t-shirt blank
- o Infusible Ink Transfer Sheet
- o White cardstock (80 lb)
- o Scissors
- o Cricut Maker or Cricut Explore cutting machine
- o Cricut EasyPress 2 or Cricut EasyPress
- o Sheets of butcher paper
- o Lint roller

**Directions:**

- o Step 1. On a green Regular Grip sheet with the color liner side down and color side up, put an Infusible Ink Transfer Mat.
- o Step 2. To get the free cut file you have created, head over to Design space. With a mermaid costume, ideal for summer and relaxing beach days, it says, "See you later." If required, resize the template, then follow the instructions to cut. Be sure the template is mirrored!

Choose "Browse All Materials," then "Infusible Ink Transfer Sheet." Change the key to "Custom" first when working with the Cricut Explore machine. Load the blade and mat into the machine, then click the Go" lighting button to cut.

o Step 3. Remove from the sheet the trimmed Infusible Ink Transfer board. For another task, use scissors to cut through the cut layout and keep the remaining transfer sheet. When treating Infusible Ink Transfer Sheets, make sure that there is no oil or sweat on your palms, leading to trouble while using the ink. Roll the cut layout carefully such that the cut items are easy to see as they continue to detach. Using your hands, extract the negative components from around the design to expose only the design on the liner. Rather than weed vinyl and iron-on. You will appreciate that it is way simpler to weed Infusible Ink Transfer Sheets. The transition sheets are much stronger and very can be readily peeled off! Trim the liner if you needed to so that it is not broader than the heat plate by EasyPress.

o Step 4. To eliminate tiny dirt and fibers from the coat, use a lint roller. This may sound pointless, but do not miss it! And quite minor debris in the transfer will cause imperfections, and we obviously do not want that. Cover the shirt (which is bigger than the Easy Press heat plate) with butcher paper. In each box of Infusible Ink Transfer Sheets, Butcher paper fits in.

- Step 5. Essential- Preheat the region where the transfer can eliminate excess liquid and wrinkles. For this task, push it for 15 seconds at 385 degrees. Allow the shirt to cool fully after removing the butcher paper.

- Step 6. With the design faced down and the transparent liner on top, on the shirt, put the cut ink transfer design sheet. Cover with butcher paper that is broader than the heat plate from EasyPress. For 40 seconds, set the EasyPress2, then put the EasyPress at 385 degrees over the design for 40 seconds. At this moment, do not shift your hand! You want it all to be good, so the transfer does not shift at all. Raise the EasyPress 2 steadily without shaking the stack or the butcher paper as the EasyPress buzzes. Let it cool the design. Typically, the design would come straight out, but if it does not, make careful to extract it with tongs and not the fingertips. When cool, you will carefully remove that butcher paper then the filler with the design. You do not want your shirt to get destroyed!

## 6.2 Infusible Ink Coaster Tutorial

**Supplies:**

o   Standard Grip Mat

o   Cricut EasyPress Mat

o   Infusible Ink Transfer Sheet

o   White cardstock (80 lb)

o   Lint-free cloth

o   Scissors

o   Cricut Maker or Cricut Explore cutting machine

- Heat Resistant Tape

- Cricut Square Coaster Blank

- Butcher paper.

- Cricut EasyPress 2 or Cricut EasyPress

- Directions:

- Step 1. On Standard green Grip mat with the paint side up and the liner side down, put an Infusible Ink Transfer Sheet.

- Stage 2. To get the free cut file, you developed, head over to Design space. If required, resize the design, then follow the instructions to cut. Be sure the template is replicated! "Choose "Browse all materials," then "Infusible Ink Transfer Sheet." First, change the dial to "Custom" while using a Cricut Explore machine. Insert the blade and mat into the machine, then click the glowing "Go" button to cut this.

- Step 3. Remove the Transfer Sheet sliced out from the mat. For another task, use scissors to cut through the cut design to keep the transfer sheet's remainder. Roll the cut design carefully such that the cut parts are easy to view and begin to split. With your hands, extract the negative parts from around the design, such that just the design is exposed on the liner. Trim the liner if you need to so that it is not wider than the heat plate of EasyPress.

- Step 4. Set your EasyPress 2 for 60 seconds and 400 degrees. Using a lint-free cloth to clear from the coaster some small particles of dirt. To protect it, shield your EasyPress Mat along with white cardstock. Also, with the liner side up on the coaster, put your design face down. To tape the design down so it remains in place, it is preferred to use heat-resistance tape. Position the coaster on the mat and cardstock. Use butcher paper to cover the coaster (that is added in each Infusible Ink Transfer Sheets box).

- Step 5. Using EasyPress 2 to press for 60 seconds at 400 degrees without any stress. Lift it gently off the coaster as the machine beeps. Try not to transfer the butcher paper beneath it or something else.

- Alert- The coaster is going to be hot! Before pressing, avoid the impulse to touch and just let it cool down. Slowly extract that butcher paper, design, and tape from the coaster until it is cold.

## 6.3 Handmade Paper Flower Corsage

For Prom, these will also look fantastic: select colors to compliment your Prom gown and put them in a keepsake box. A (stored correctly) paper flower corsage can last for many years that can be used again. If you get the best of it, producing paper flowers is very easy.

**Supplies:**

o Scissors

o Ribbon or pins

o Glue

o Cardstock (in your color choice for flowers and leaves)

o Free template

**Directions:**

o Step1. Print a template and split the flower template on your card stock color option.

o Step2. Spray the paper slightly with water (it will enable you to curl the paper into the forms you want and fold that paper sheet to form shapes.

o Step3. On each flower segment and leaves, stick the tabs together, and allow them to dry.

o Step4. Using watercolors or labels, apply colored edges (optional). Glue together every leaf and petal to shape a flower and let it dry.

o Step5. If you make a wrist corsage, adhere the completed flower to the ribbon after cutting its appropriate size. Position it at the back of the flower using pins for giving as a present. Wrap the corsage in a keepsake box or a cellophane bag.

## 6.4 Coffee Mug

It is simpler than it seems to make Cricut Coffee Mugs! This is a fun project by Cricut Explore Air that an inexperienced can build. If you think that Cricut Mugs are safe for the dishwasher, no, they're not. If you send these mugs as

Christmas presents from Cricut, make sure you send a message to the receiver that these mugs only have to be hand-washed. The trouble with dishwasher cleaning is that certain dishwashers have incredibly high-temperature settings that can melt off the durable vinyl. It is safer to wash and dry with warm soapy water while you are using Cricut vinyl on the mugs.

Supplies:

o   Cricut Explore/Silhouette cutting machine

o   Permanent Vinyl

o   Transfer Tape

o   12 x 12 Cricut Cutting Mat

o   SVG file (get it free below or use your own image)

o   Coffee Mugs

**Directions:**

o Step1-Collect supplies.

o Step2-Use the Silhouette or Cricut cutting machine to cut the SVG picture (or your picture), then weed the picture. Depending on the height of your mug, size the picture differently.

o Step3-To the weeded picture, add the transfer tape, press the image tightly on the mug while peeling back the vinyl paper.

o Step4-Peel the transfer tape back then you are done!

## 6.5 FAIRY HOUSE CARD

Give this card to a beloved one to rejoice, or hold it for yourselves! The card folds horizontally so that you can slide it into an envelope of 5" x 7", then pops open to expose the loveliest little fairy home! To see inside, open the little flap. The card has too many descriptions.

## Supplies:

- 12" x 12" Pink cardstock

- Tape

- 12" x 12' Tan cardstock

- Glue

- 12" x 12" Brown cardstock

- Spray adhesive

## Directions:

- Step 1: Uploading and Ungrouping.

- Step 2: Adjust each color's top layer to Score.

- Step 3: Choose the cut layer and score for each paint, and press attach.

- After cutting the parts, customize the front of the house

as you see fit. Around the walls, the circles fall. Small accessories will go as far as they fit. Just be sure that none of the score lines are protected. To get the little parts to fit neatly towards the house's front, you can use the Spray Mount. If you are going to bring something inside the house on the walls, do that now, too.

o   Step 4: Fold the house carefully along the lines of the score.

o   Step 5: Put adhesive on the thin tab that sticks out of the house's back and tie this to the left side of the house. Fold it flat and allow the flattened one to dry. This means that the card folds flat and will not buckle later on.

o   Step 6: Fold the tabs on the staircase piece, put adhesive on the tabs, and place them in the home from the bottom. However, you might choose to put it wherever. The key element is to guarantee that the staircase is adjacent to the front door and that the tabs are placed directly over each other, guaranteeing that the card will fold flat without an issue.

o   Tip: If you are trying to hide the mouse from the back of the card in its little trap, stick it to the back of the staircase so that it is noticeable as you peek through the mouse hole.

o Adhesive the rectangular parts with some accessories, decorations, or notes you want. Rollback the tabs on the rectangle's parts, then slip it down the staircase from the bottom into the house. For a far more three-dimensional look and allow some gap between each part

o Fold the rooftop hinge such that each tab goes from the others in the reverse direction.

o Place adhesive on the small pieces of the hinge triangle and bind them on the house roof's points. On the rear end of the roof tips, the triangle parts fall.

o Place on the roof any flowers or decorations you will need, then fold along the score line in half. Ensure the roof is folded well. To set the crease, rub your fingernail over the side.

o Attach the two tabs to the roof's hinge, then bind the roof to the tabs. To put it in order, fold the house flat and push the roof down on the tabs.

o Yeah, that is it! You have got an amazingly Fairy House Card already!

## 6.6 BIRTHDAY GARLAND BANNER

### Supplies

o  Card stock in multiple colors

o  Twine, string or ribbon

o  Cricut machine and Cricut Design Space account

### Directions

o  Upload to Design Space the birthday cupcake SVG.

o  Resize as required.

o  Slice several parts into various shades.

o   Remove as required from the weed and mat.

o  String with twine or ribbon and showcase as desired.

## 6.7 Rock Art

With vinyl word-painting, make fun rock art that you can cut out easily. For family or party events, this Cricut project works ideally. Everybody can paint their rocks and decorate them how they wish. Then go for a ride and leave the rocks of your art for others to discover.

**Supplies**

- Rocks – washed and dried

- Sealer – You can use Mod Podge

- Paint and paint brushes

- Permanent Vinyl

- Cricut machine and Cricut Design Space account

## Directions

o Paint your rocks as much as you like and enable them to dry. Whether using seal or gloss paint the painted rock to make the vinyl stick to the surface better until adding the vinyl.

o Using your Cricut design space and Cricut machine, cut out the vinyl word art. By one of my design sets accessible through Cricut Library. Any font, or just an uploaded SVG design, will work.

o When the vinyl design has been added, lock it.

Notes on vinyl use. You might struggle with transfer tape, but the easiest course to go is not always with transfer tape. However, light grip is preferred if you are successful at utilizing transfer tape, but often the vinyl does not want to adhere to a painted rock straight away. Using vinyl designs is preferred that pull the backing off like a sticker. So, try sticker if transfer tape is not really your thing.

Using several shades of colors to paint rock art at once.

## 6.8 Floral Nail Decals

Cut out tiny flower nail decals in minutes with your Cricut! With your Cricut and Vinyl, start dressing your fingernails with

DIY nail art that you create. You can add adorable designs in a nail present package or share them for a fun community manicure game. Nail decals from vinyl are easy to create and enjoyable to use!

- You can use whatever color of vinyl you like as far as it cuts using your Cricut machine to produce one's vinyl flower decals. The durable adhesive lasts longer, but still, the vinyl removal can cut and stick.

**Supplies**

o  Top Coat nail polish

o  Vinyl you can cut

o  Design canvas in order to help you begin.

o  Cricut machine and Cricut Design Space account

**Directions**

o  Go to the design Space.

o  Resize the designs of the art to your desired scale.

o  To remove your floral designs from the vinyl of the selection, obey the on-screen directions.

o  Ensure your nails are clean and dry to add the vinyl decals to your nails. If you would prefer, apply a polish shade and or top coat first. With the decal added, press firmly in place. To hold the vinyl in place, add a topcoat.

Tip: To seal the decal to your finger, make sure to use a topcoat to allow it last longer.

## 6.9 Fall Mantel

By using this DIY Fall Mantel with a Fall Art Cut File, create a nice focal point built for you using pictures, florals, and this latest fall SVG art style. You may customize the art to print or cut in any color you might like with your Cricut. This Fall Art DIY is great for all of your projects with Fall Cricut.

- By using your Cricut Computer, you may customize your lovely fall mantel using fabric or paper. Attach the SVG file and begin to create creating! To suit your design aesthetic, you can change the look and build a mantel that is ideal for your own house!

**Supplies**

- Fall Leaf SVG by Jen Goode – Free download below
- Printer

- o Ribbon, crepe paper ribbon can also work.

- o Optional: black marker, paper, wood slice and twine.

- o Copper Cricut Pen (Optional)

- o Cardstock – white

- o Cricut Machine

- o Adhesive (You can used hot glue)

**Directions**

- o Personalize the shades, sizes, and design accents by uploading the SVG file to Cricut Design Room. To print and cut the art, obey the on-screen directions. Optionally, you may opt to use colorful paper to cut all the art.

- o Use a strip of ribbon to stretch the size of your mantel, leaving either edge with around 6-8" excess."

- o Arrange the cut art on the ribbon as you might like and stick to it in place. Before using adhesive, be sure to place something under the ribbon to protect the ribbon from sticking to the flat surface. Enable it to dry out.

- o Apply a ribbon around your mantel.

If you choose to do further combinations of your leaves, create copies of each leaf in Cricut Design Space and flip or copy them. For each art style, you can adjust the shades as well as the drawing line. Customize the art you would like, though.

## 6.10 Advent Calendar

Create your perfect Advent Calendar with printables and cut files that are simple to use. Customize the appearance, and in minutes, apply your shades and design. You can create one for the entire family, or you can choose to make one for all!

There are two pieces of the printable kit and other extras. This little box comes with a free PDF that can be printed or cut, and use the SVG and import and cut with your Cricut to your Design Space account. The tiny numbers are also accessible as PDF and PNG to download. You should upload the PNG to Design Space and then turn the Design Cut to Print.

## Supplies

o  Cardstock

o  Printer

o  Ribbon or yarn

o  Cricut machine

## Directions

o  Cut and set the boxes.

o  Cut out numbers and designs and add them to one of the tiny boxes as accents.

o   Fill every box. String it up with a ribbon and make a loop with a short bow.

o  String ribbon and yarn on the wall or board.

o   Clip every box to the hanging ribbon.

# Chapter 7: Pros and Cons

## 7.1 Pro

- Professional cutting level.

- No requirement for a distinct fabric cutter.

- Massive library for sewing patterns.

- Significant enhancements on Explore Air 2.

- Faster production of professional cuts in a thorough way.

- People without technical expertise would be happily surprised by how simple it is to use the Cricut Explore One, mainly because no additional software can be installed.

- The guidelines are relatively straightforward, and the modelling tools required to build and render your crafts can be downloaded via Cricut's website for free.

- This implies that without installing software on each computer you have; you can work on your tasks at any time and from everywhere.

- You can build and upload designs from your device, iPhone, or iPad wirelessly with the Bluetooth adapter.

- This allows you full flexibility to switch and print from room to room and to cut down on your home's wire clutter.

- For beginners, the Cricut Explore One is a perfect Cricut machine since it is so simple to set up and all the functions can be quickly learned, making it a popular option for new craftsmen for a cutting machine.

- Excellent cutting ability due to the rotary blade that cuts like butter through the cloth.

- You would be able to compose and cut at the same time with a Cricut Explore One, thereby saving you considerable time making crafts. You may also build folding lines for particular tasks such as making packages, cards, and 3D items with the scoring stylus.

- Despite its latest additions, its price tag of under $500 is nothing short of astounding.

- A true game-changer is the rich sewing catalogue that comes with this unit.

- Thanks to its turbocharged motor and cutting-edge tech, this machine is a true workhorse.

- This amazing machine will absolutely learn the most intricate designs. The Cricut's thorough work is superior to the output of the Silhouette, but frankly, the gap is so minuscule that it is almost not worth remembering.

- If you are concerned that this machine will become outdated, you will be in for a real surprise, all thanks to its innovative design.

- The system is automated to quickly detect whether or not you are dealing with the correct blade.

- A machine for life

- Extraordinarily versatile

- Amazing tool capability

## 7.2 Cons

- Cricut Production Space software is a bit clunky

- Limited cutting space

- For around $149, The Cricut Explore One retails. Although a used machine may be found for less for beginners or those looking to play with one before making a significant investment. Delivering professional cuts quicker in a thorough way

- Excellent cutting ability due to the rotary blade that cuts like butter across the cloth

- Given its latest additions, its price tag of under $500 is nothing short of astounding.

- Craft materials may become very pricey, so it will be prudent to research where to buy supplies that work into the budget with that in mind. At bargain stores like Dollar Tree or online via Amazon would be a decent place to start from

- A true game-changer is the rich sewing catalogue that comes with this unit.

- Thanks to its turbocharged motor and cutting-edge tech, this machine is a true workhorse.

- For premium templates, cartridges, fonts, and other items such as the scoring stylus that do not arrive with your Cricut machine, you may have to pay extra.

- If you are concerned that this machine will become outdated, you will be in for a real surprise, all thanks to its revolutionary architecture.

- The system is automated to quickly detect whether or not you are dealing with the correct blade.

- Since it is cloud-focused, the Cricut Modelling program is slow. The cloud relies on internet speed to work. While designing, there might be a small pause that is irritating for someone who likes efficiency and hates waiting.

# Chapter 8: The Cricut Community

## 8.1 What is Cricut Community?

There is nothing better than the joy of having built something wonderful, exceptional, and perfect in your life for yourself or anyone special. The only other thing you may dream of that can top an artistic high is to discuss what you have created with other crafters. The act of connecting brings your ideas to a whole different level, so other designers will be motivated to achieve something they might never have achieved on their own. The creative thinking YOU can inspire in others truly has no end.

In the Design space, the latest Projects and Profiles Collaboration capabilities are only the start of your initiatives to intensify the creativity of those utilizing products from Cricut. Think about the last gathering that you were organizing. Or the gift you have created. Or the sign you have designed. Someone else in the world of Cricut is searching for the very thing that you created for their own creation as a starting point. Give a hand to them through Cricut Community.! And like all aspects of life, your kindness would come back tenfold to you.

## 8.2 How to create an account at Cricut Community?

In Cricut Design Space, the profile feature makes it easier for you to publicly share your designs with other Cricut users. In order to display step-by-step guidance for building your Profile, pick your platform below.

Remember: The Profile feature is accessible on Design Space's iOS and Mac/Windows platforms. On Android, it is not accessible yet.

- To design your Cricut Group profile, proceed to design.cricut.com.

- Enter your ID and password for Cricut, then select Sign In.

- In the home screen, in the upper left corner, select the three-bar option.

- Press the 'View Profile link.'

- Press Edit Profile on the Profile tab to include the avatar picture and things you want other Cricut users to know about you.

- To start uploading your profile photo, select 'Change profile photo.'

- To search your machine for the picture you want to use, press Upload Picture. Use the slider after you have selected the picture to resize the photo and reposition it as desired.

- To switch to the Profile page, press 'Done.'

- If needed, in the 'About Me' portion, add details that you would like Cricut members to know regarding you. To save these updates to your Profile, press Save.

- Those projects will display on your Profile when you share tasks with the Cricut group. In the Design space, the designs that are shown on this website would be accessible. If you have not shared tasks with the Cricut Group, your profile page will show five blank project boxes.

- To make corrections or to see which tasks are accessible to everyone, move to your profile page at any moment.

Note: Profile feature is available at Mac, Windows and iOS platforms of Design Space. But it is not available on Android yet.

## 8.3 How to find projects at Cricut Community?

Using the powerful search engine of Cricut to search for tens of thousands of projects supported by fellow Cricut crafters.

Note: Community Project Quest is only accessible in Design Space in the browser currently.

- Navigate and sign in with the Cricut password and ID to Cricut Design Room.

- Second, navigate to the tab for projects. Click 'View All' on any task ribbon on the Home page to get to the Tasks list.

- From the drop-down list, choose Cricut Community

- In the search section, enter keywords to locate the projects you are involved in. Here are several quest tips:

- The more detailed, the better. To aid us in providing the most impressive information, use multiple keywords. There is no requirement for quotation marks around a statement or the usage of other symbols.

- Pluralization and Capitalization? No issues! You can search for all types of keywords automatically.

- You can search everywhere! You can check for matches in project names, descriptions, and tags if you type a keyword in the search section.

Tip: The more data you attach to your project tags, titles, and explanation while sharing it with the Cricut Community, the more likely others can find it. Add a comprehensive project title, complete project tags, and project description for better performance.

## 8.4 How to share projects with Cricut Community?

Create your Design Space profile from either our iOS app or from a web browser to get started. This is as basic as posting a casual photo and composing a short bio that explains your favorite crafting practices. Then upload projects for all to admire your Profile! This method is simple, and a photo of your project is all you need.

- In Design Space, visit the 'My Projects page' and choose any project you might like to share with the Cricut group. To access the form, click on Sharing, upload your photo, then add a description. The project is ready to be shared.

- Now you can share your project for everyone to appreciate, on your preferred Facebook group or

Pinterest page. In Design Space, other crafters may be able to open it up because if they want to do anything later; they will favorite it for later.

# Conclusion

The Cricut Maker comes out as a fairly successful machine, evaluating the merits against the demerits (its advantages heavily outweigh the disadvantages). Among the factors is that this machine is so cool are its 4kg cutting capacity, vast pattern library, and innovative rotary blade. However, on the other side, the choice to continue the Design Space software refuse it a few points due to the restricted cutting space. Can you craft, or do you find yourself in a place where you have to cut? If the reaction to do that is yes, you will profit completely by getting a Cricut. With several crafters out there, Cricut is a fantasy come true. For various items, such as card making, home decor, etc., you may use it. Also, Cricut would be your strongest and most trusted cutting assistant if you deal with fabrics and cut loads of cloth in various sizes.

This machine is awarded a well-deserved 4.9 on a scale of 5. Cricut Machine is strongly recommended to any creative artist trying to take a step higher with their passion. So, if you want your imaginations, fascinations, and ideas to come into reality, then you should not wait a moment and get your very own Cricut Machine. You will surely have a very amazing time making customized crafts and bringing your ideas to life.